Dictionary of
Computer
Terms

BROCKHAMPTON PRESS
LONDON

This edition published 1996 by Brockhampton Press,
a member of the Hodder Headline PLC Group

ISBN 1 86019 301 3

Printed and bound in India

A

abort to cancel or terminate a process or procedure while it is in progress.

accelerator board an adapter for the computer containing a more advanced microprocessor than the one already in the computer. Adding an accelerator can speed up the computer generally or can speed up a particular function such as the graphics display.

access to locate and retrieve the information, whether in the form of data or PROGRAM instructions, stored on a disk or in a computer. Nowadays the term usually refers to the amount of time it takes to transfer information from one source to another, and is called the **access time**. It is measured in nanoseconds (ns) for memory chips and in milliseconds (ms) for data transfer from the hard disk. Typical access times for hard disks on personal computers range between the fast (9ms) and the slow at around 100ms. The access time is determined by the time required for the disk heads to move to the correct track (the seek time), and then to settle down (the settle time) and the time needed for the sector to move under the head (latency).

acoustic coupler cradles that hold a telephone handset and allow MODEMS to communicate through the telephone.

active cell the cell in a SPREADSHEET in which the cursor is currently positioned, allowing a number or formula to be entered.

active matrix display a liquid crystal display (LCD) in

7

which each of the display's electrodes is under the control of it own transistor. Active matrix displays are more expensive than the lower resolution PASSIVE MATRIX DISPLAYS.

active window in an APPLICATION PROGRAM or OPERATING SYSTEM that can display multiple windows, the active window is the one that accepts commands or typing and is indicated by a coloured bar at the top of the window.

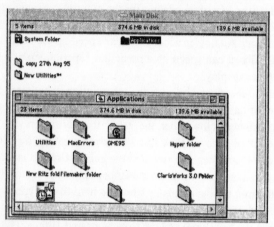

The active window has a shaded title bar

Ada a programming language designed for US Government operations. It is a high-level structured language developed around 1980 that is designed to be readable for ease of maintenance.

adapter card a card complete with electronic components that plugs into the computer's main circuit board with the aim of providing enhanced capabilities. Adapter cards can be used to provide high quality graphics, modems, etc.

ADb *see* APPLE DESKTOP BUS.

add in program a small program that is designed to complement an application and add to the capabilities of the host application.

address a location in a computer system that is identified by a name or code. The address is specified by the program or the user.

address bus an electronic channel linking the microprocessor to the random access memory (*see* RAM) along which the addresses of memory locations are transmitted.

Adobe Type Manager (ATM) a program that smoothes out the edges of type for presentation on the screen. This is especially useful where the printer prints exactly what is on the screen. If it looks good on the screen it will look good in print.

AI *see* ARTIFICIAL INTELLIGENCE.

AIX (Advanced Interactive eXecutive) a variant of the UNIX operating system developed by IBM primarily for their workstations.

alert box a WINDOW appearing on a screen providing a warning that an error has occurred or the command chosen may result in lost work.

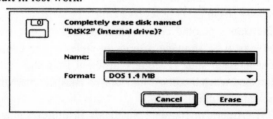

Alert box associated with an erase disk command

algorithm 10

algorithm a set of straightforward logical mathematical steps that, if followed, provide a solution to a problem.

alias a representation of an original document or file that can be used as if it was the original. An alias's name appears in italics. An alias is not a copy of the file but a small file that directs the computer to the original file. Using an alias can assist in file storage and retrieval.

aliasing *see* JAGGIES.

alignment *see* READ/WRITE HEAD ALIGNMENT; TEXT ALIGNMENT.

alphanumeric character any keyboard character that can be typed, such as A to Z in either uppercase or lowercase, numbers 1 to 10 and punctuation marks.

Amstrad a computer company founded by Alan Sugar. It made its name with a word processing computer that sold well, mainly because of its low price. However, it was rapidly superseded by generations of PERSONAL COMPUTERS.

analogue the opposite of DIGITAL. An analogue signal varies continuously to reflect the changes in the state of the quantity being measured, e.g. sound waves vary continually. A thermometer is an analogue measurement device, and as the temperature varies so does the height of the mercury. On the other hand, digital signals are either on or off.

AND *see* FORMULA; LOGICAL OPERATOR.

animation a graphic creation that gives the impression of movement by showing a series of slides on the computer screen. Each slide is slightly different from the previous slide and when the images are played back fast enough, the movement appears smooth.

ANSI (American National Standards Institute) a non-governmental organization founded in 1981 to approve the specification of data processing standards in the USA. It is also responsible for the definition of HIGH-LEVEL PROGRAM-MING LANGUAGES.

anti-virus program a program that checks for the existence of a VIRUS and informs the user if there is one present on the computer's secondary storage. The virus is identified either by the existence of the virus codes or by identifying the effect of the virus (e.g. corrupted files).

APL (A Program Language) a HIGH-LEVEL PROGRAMMING LAN-GUAGE designed for handling engineering and mathematical functions and as a notation for communication between mathematicians. It is quick, efficient and well suited to WHAT IF applications.

Apple Computer, Inc. a pioneering and innovative company in the information industry. It creates solutions based on easy to use PERSONAL COMPUTERS, SERVERS, PERIPHERALS, SOFTWARE and PERSONAL DIGITAL ASSISTANTS. Based in California, Apple develops, manufactures, licenses and markets products, technologies and services for education, business, consumers and for industrial scientific, and government organizations in over 140 countries. It is one of the largest manufacturers of personal computers in the world. The brand name of its range of computers is MACINTOSH.

Apple desktop bus (ADb) a standard INTERFACE for Apple computers that allows connection of input devices such as keyboards, mice, graphics tablets and trackballs to all Macintosh computers. Up to 16 ADb devices can be connected to the computer, which can receive data at approximately 4.5 kilobits (i.e. 4500 bits) per second.

AppleShare a NETWORK OPERATING SYSTEM that converts an

Apple Macintosh computer into a file SERVER for a network. The server can be accessed by the network as if it were an added HARD DISK.

AppleTalk a program that connects computers and other hardware such as printers together in a LOCAL AREA NETWORK. Every Apple Computer has Appletalk network facilities built in.

application program a computer program that performs specific tasks such as letter writing, statistical analysis, design, etc. Application programs work with the OPERATING SYSTEM to control peripheral devices such as printers.

archive a store of files (either PROGRAM or DATA) that is kept as a backup in case the original files are corrupted or damaged. An archived file is often stored in a compressed format (*see* COMPRESS) in order to use up less disk space.

arithmetic operator a symbol that indicates which arithmetical operation to perform. In a SPREADSHEET, arithmetic operators are used to compile formulae for adding (+), subtracting (–), multiplying (*) or dividing (/) the contents of cells to obtain the desired result.

array a form in which data is stored by computer programs. An array is a table of data. The data is accessed by naming the array and then by the X and Y coordinates.

artificial intelligence (AI) the ability of an artificial mechanism to exhibit intelligent behaviour by modifying its actions through reasoning and learning from experience. Artificial intelligence is also the name of the research discipline in which artificial mechanisms that exhibit intelligence are developed and studied. It was first discussed by the British mathematician Alan Turing, who is regarded as one of the founders of the subject. In recent years artificial intelligence has been used in the development of expert systems that use knowledge-based information to make seemingly rational decisions. However, this rationale is limited to a specific knowledge area. It is generally accepted that AI has not met its objectives and the necessary solutions are probably many, many years away.

ascending order a method of sorting data in a list with the result that the data is arranged from 1 to 10 or A to Z. Descending order reverses the sort order.

1	.	A
2	/	a
3	r	B
6	t	b
8	u	C
15	w	c
22	y	D
44	^	d
66	2	E
75	5	e

Each column is sorted in ascending order

ASCII (American Standard Code for Information Interchange) one of several standard sets of codes devised in 1968 that define the way information is transferred from one computer to another. It is one method of representing BINARY code, whereby specific binary patterns are represented by alphanumeric codes. The standard ASCII code contains 96 upper and lower case characters and 32 control characters that are not displayed.

assembly language a LOW-LEVEL PROGRAMMING LANGUAGE that is based on instructions that relate directly to the processing chip. (*See also* HIGH-LEVEL PROGRAMMING LANGUAGE.)

assistant a series of steps in an application program, similar to a WIZARD, that assists the user to create a particular document style such as mailing lists, advertising flyers, newsletters, envelopes, etc.

asynchronous communication a commonly used mode of transmitting data over telephone lines. The two communicating systems are not synchronized and characters are sent or received one at a time. The start and ending of a stream of data are denoted by a START BIT and a stop bit.

ATM *see* ADOBE TYPE MANAGER.

Auto CAD a widely used but very expensive CAD program.

auto dial a feature of most communications programs in which the program automatically dials the appropriate phone number and makes a connection with the answering computer.

auto dial/auto answer modem a MODEM that is able to generate tones to dial the receiving computer and also to answer the telephone and establish a link when a call is received.

auxiliary storage another term for SECONDARY STORAGE.

auto save a utility that regularly saves the work being done on a computer onto the hard disk. It is important to save work regularly otherwise there is a risk of loss of work because of, for example, a power or computer failure. The auto save utility sets the computer to save at specific intervals, allowing the user to progress with productive work.

B

BABT (British Approvals Board for Telecommunications) an organization that approves all devices for use with the public telephone network, e.g. MODEMS, FAX cards and SERVERS (not ACOUSTIC COUPLERS).

background task some computer operating systems allow more than one task to be completed at a time. The main or high priority procedure is carried out in the FOREGROUND and lower priority procedures are carried out in the background.

backlit screen a type of display mostly used in NOTEBOOK or LAPTOP COMPUTERS. The display uses LCD technology to light the display behind the text. The text is contrasted against the background.

backspace a keyboard key that moves the CURSOR to the left, deleting any previously typed characters.

backup a copy of a program or data file that is kept for ARCHIVE purposes usually on a removable floppy or hard disk.

backup utility an easy to use program that automatically makes a copy of the main storage disk of a computer. The copy or backup is usually made onto tape, optical disk or floppy disks. The better backup utility programs copy only the files that have been updated since the previous backup, thus saving time and disk space.

backward compatible an application program that works

not only with the most recent version of an operating system but also with previous versions.

bad sector a part of a disk (HARD DISK or FLOPPY DISK) that cannot be used to record data. Bad sectors can be generated in manufacturing, caused by damage in handling the disk or by dust. When a bad sector is identified, the disk should be discarded if it is a floppy or reformatted if it is a hard disk.

bandwidth a measure of the range of frequencies that can pass through an INTEGRATED CIRCUIT. The greater the bandwidth the more information that can pass through the circuit.

bar code a series of printed vertical bars of differing widths that represent numbers. These codes are printed on virtually every supermarket product and are then used by appropriate software to identify the product for stock control and sales pricing. Bar codes are also found on books and other publications and many other items.

A representation of a bar code

BASIC (Beginner's All-purpose Symbolic Instruction Code) one of the most popular computer programming languages. It was developed at Dartmouth College in the USA in 1964 by John Kemeny and Thomas Kurtz. BASIC is available on a wide range of computer platforms and is one of the easiest languages in which to program. It is normally an interpretative language, with each statement being interpreted and executed as it is encountered. It can also be a compiled language, with all the statements being compiled into machine code before execution. Early versions of BASIC were criticized for not encouraging structured programming. New versions of BASIC, i.e. Visual Basic, are very powerful indeed.

BAT the common extension used at the end of a BATCH FILE name.

batch file a file containing DOS commands that is accessed by typing the file name at the DOS prompt. This file type has the extension .BAT.

batch processing a type of computer operation that processes a series or batch of commands at one time without user intervention. A BATCH FILE, for example, processes a group of DOS commands on start-up to assist the user.

baud a measure of telecommunications transmission speed denoting the number of discrete signal elements that can be transmitted per second. Devised by a 19th-century French telecommunications pioneer, J.M. Baudot, the **baud rate** is the standard way of representing information in telex and telegraph communications. It commonly refers to the changes in signal frequency per second, and not BITS per second unless at low baud rates (300) where it is equal to bits per second. At higher rates, the number of bits per second transmitted is higher than the baud rate, and one change in the electrical state of the circuit represents more than one bit of data. This means that 1200 bits per second can be sent at 600 baud.

bells and whistles the advanced features that an application program contains. Most users find that they regularly use only a small percentage of the features of a full-featured program, whether it is a word processor, a SPREADSHEET or a graphics program. This is an argument for buying a low-featured program, which is usually substantially cheaper in price and yet meets most requirements.

benchmark a measurement standard used to compare the performance of different computers and equipment. Standard measures of processor speeds do not take account of the speed of other devices such as disk drives or communications, whereas modern benchmark tests take all factors of the computer system into account.

Bernoulli a type of DISK DRIVE, usually holding over 20 megabytes of data, that uses removable cartridges.

beta testing the final stage of testing of a computer program before it is released for general sale. The testing is usually performed by a number of selected users who have knowledge of, and skill in, using the particular type of application.

Bezier curve a style of curve that depends on vector forces of power and angle to determine its shape. In computer graphics these curves are manipulated by control handles at the midpoints of a curve.

bidirectional a term to describe a device, usually a printer, that is capable of printing from right to left as well as from left to right. There are also bidirectional printer ports, capable of sending and receiving data. SERIAL cables are bidirectional, as they are capable of transmitting and receiving information.

Big Blue the colloquial name given to IBM (International Business Machines), one of the largest computer companies in the world.

binary the language of all computers in which all numbers, letters and special characters are represented by 1 and 0. It is called base two notation. (*See* BINARY NUMBERS).

binary digit *see* BIT.

binary numbers the use of a base notation of two compared with a base notation of 10 in normal decimal numbers and 16 in a HEXADECIMAL numbering system. In base two, there are only two states, 0 or 1 ('on' or 'off').

BIOS (Basic Input Output System) a code that resides on a ROM chip and controls basic hardware operations such as the PROCESSORS dealings with disk drives, displays, and keyboard.

bit (Binary digIT) the smallest unit of information in a digital computer. It has a value of 0 or 1 that represents yes/no and either/or choices. A collection of eight bits is called a BYTE.

bitmap a method of storing graphics information in memory in which a BIT is devoted to each PIXEL (picture element) on screen. A bitmap contains a bit for each point or dot on a video display, and can allow for fine RESOLUTION because each point on the display can be addressed. Unfortunately, bit-mapped graphics require a great deal of memory, often in excess of one megabyte. A BIT-MAPPED font is a font for screen and/or printer in which every character is made up of a pattern of dots. To allow display or printing, a full record must be kept in the computer's memory. Again, this is a memory-intensive process.

bits per second (bps) a measure of speed of data transmission, especially in connection with the performance of MO-DEMS.

board *see* CARD.

block a selection of information that can be dealt with by one series of commands. For example, in SPREADSHEET applications a block of information can be selected and copied to another part of the sheet.

boilerplate a standard passage of text used in memos, reports or letters. The passage is often stored in a SCRAPBOOK and pasted into a document as required. Letterheads are examples of a boilerplate that can easily be retrieved when required. Contracts of employment can also be saved in a standard format and recalled as required. Only minor amendments then need to be made to the document before printing.

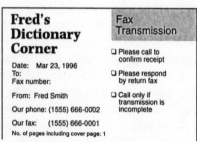

An example of a boilerplate

bold a style of text that adds emphasis to a character by making it darker and heavier than normal type. The headwords in this book are printed in **bold type**.

bomb an unexpected termination of an application, similar to a CRASH. This can indicate a serious problem with the hardware, but most often it is caused by a software conflict.

bootstrapping a program routine designed to make a computer ready for use. To 'boot the system' or INITIALIZE it is to make it ready for normal use. In modern computers booting the system loads its OPERATING SYSTEM into memory and prepares it to run application programs. Within the ROM of a computer is a program that is started when the power is switched on, and this tells the computer to search for the computer's operating system. This is called a **cold boot**. A WARM BOOT is achieved either by pressing the reset button on newer IBM computers and compatibles or by pressing the Ctrl/Alt/Del keys simultaneously. This is usually done to unlock the system.

bps *see* BITS PER SECOND.

branch a section of a program that causes the program to divert to a subroutine when certain criteria are met. On completion of the subroutine the program returns to the main trunk. The term can also apply to a section of a DIRECTORY.

broad band an ANALOGUE communications method using high BANDWIDTH. Broad band communications operate at high speeds and can be sent over long distances.

browse to display records in a format suitable for quick on-screen review and editing.

bubblejet *see* INKJET.

buffer an electronic memory storage device that is used for temporary storage of data passing in or out of the computer. A common use for a buffer is as a temporary holding area between a slow-moving device and a fast-moving device, i.e. between a computer and a printer. A buffer therefore allows different parts of the computer system to operate at optimum speeds.

bug a mistake—a hardware or software error. The term was first coined in the early days of computing when a butterfly was found to have caused a malfunction in an early Mark I computer. A programming error may be serious and can cause the computer to perform incorrectly or even crash.

bulletin board a computer service set up by organizations or clubs with the aim of providing or exchanging information. It is accessed through a MODEM and telephone lines and can provide entertainment services as well as information.

bundled software software that is provided with a computer as part of the overall purchase price. For example, some computer manufacturers would like their products to be seen as easy to use and so they try to cut out the difficulties that a new user associates with setting up programs. To achieve this, the manufacturer bundles software that is already set up in the computer system. The new user can then take the machine from the box, set it up and be productive very quickly.

burn-in a period of time during which computer components are tested. CHIPS and other components have a tendency to fail early or late in their lives. Early testing of the computer, say for 48 hours, is recommended before delivery to a customer.

bus a channel through which data passes. It refers to either the **data bus** (the route data takes to the processor) or the **expansion bus** (the route by which data moves to expansion cards).

button an on-screen area in a GRAPHICAL USER INTERFACE computer that is used to select a particular command. Pointing
the mouse at the button and clicking will select the command.

A button to create a new file

byte a combination of BITS used by the computer to represent
an alphabetical character, a numerical digit or a special
character such as an accent. For example, the letter A is
represented by 01000001. A page of text will require
slightly more bytes than there are characters to store it, to
include spaces, control characters, etc. A large document
will therefore need very many bytes, and many computers
have millions of bytes (MEGABYTES) of memory. Units that
are used most often are the kilobyte and megabyte, representing 1 thousand and 1 million bytes. These are, however,
inaccurate because a kilobyte is actually 1,024 bytes (2 to
the power 2) and a megabyte 1,048,576 bytes.

C

C or **C language** a computer language developed in 1972. It is regarded as a medium-level language combining attributes from both LOW-LEVEL and HIGH-LEVEL PROGRAMMING LANGUAGES. Programs in C are easy to read, they can run very quickly, and they can run on most computers.

cache an area of the random access memory (*see* RAM) in a computer that is used as a temporary storage for frequently used data. It allows faster access to the data than if the data were held on a physical disk, thus speeding up processing.

CAD (Computer-Aided Design) special software that will create and manipulate graphics shapes in the same manner in which an architect or designer might operate. The draughtsperson can change, edit, save and reprint drawings without the problem of redrawing everything over again. Until quite recently CAD was within the realm of DEDICATED computer systems, but the increased speed, memory and processing power of modern systems means that it can be undertaken on more ordinary machines. It is used in many disciplines, including architecture, interior design, civil engineering, mechanical engineering, and so on.

CAI (Computer-Assisted Instruction) a form of teaching by computer. The CAI program leads a student through a series of tutorials, question and answer sessions, or other tests. The student can use CAI techniques to learn a wide variety of subjects, from computer programming to chess.

calculated field in a DATABASE MANAGEMENT PROGRAM a FIELD
that contains the result of a formula that may be based on
results in other fields. It may also contain dates or logical
statements; e.g., a field could be based on the formula:

$$=if(a<31, Date, 'late'),$$

which means that if the value of a is less than 31 then put
the value in Date into the field, otherwise put the word late
in the field.

calculator an on-screen utility that can be used in a fashion
similar to a hand-held calculator.

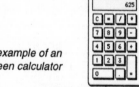

*An example of an
on-screen calculator*

CAM (Computer-Aided Manufacture) the use of computers
in manufacturing, which usually refers to the control of robots.

cancel if the user has made an error the command can be
cancelled by pressing the ESCAPE KEY in a DOS operating
system or by clicking a 'cancel' button in a GRAPHICAL USER
INTERFACE.

capacity the amount of information that can be held in a
storage device. A 3^1/$_2$-inch FLOPPY DISK will typically contain 1.4 MEGABYTES while a HARD DISK can contain up to several GIGABYTES.

card a circuit board that is made up of plastic backing with circuits etched onto the plastic. CHIPS are then attached to this base. The card is fitted into a slot in the main board of the computer. Different cards provide different functions such as communications cards, graphic accelerator cards and video capture cards.

cartridge a removable unit used as a secondary or backup storage, e.g. magnetic tape or optical disks. In a printer, it is a removable unit that contains ink that is fed to the print heads and onto the paper.

cascading windows in a GRAPHICAL USER INTERFACE environment, several windows can be open at any one time. The cascading effect is attained by overlapping the windows so that the title bar of each window is visible.

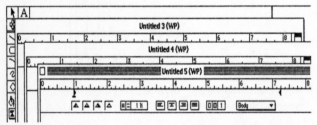

These windows cascade down the computer screen

case sensitive the ability of a program to differentiate between UPPERCASE and lowercase characters. In DOS, it does not matter whether lowercase or uppercase is used as the operating system is not case sensitive. However, in a case-sensitive search of a database, a search for 'Bill' will result in a different found set from a search for 'bill'. Some word processing programs have the capacity to convert text from lowercase to uppercase characters, and vice versa.

cathode ray tube the standard type of computer VDU that uses an electron gun to fire a beam of electrons at the phosphor screen.

CDEV (Control panel DEVice) a UTILITY PROGRAM that is designed to make a computer easier to use. Examples of CONTROL PANEL devices are for mouse settings, keyboard function keys, date and time settings, network settings, etc.

CDI (Compact Disc Interactive) a standard that refers to the design of systems for viewing audiovisual compact disks using a TV monitor and a CDI player.

CD ROM (Compact Disk Read Only Memory) a system invented by Phillips in 1983. CD ROM can store much larger amounts of data than conventional storage. Although slower than hard disks, a CD ROM will store in excess of 600 megabytes of data. They are very useful for the storage of archival data. Video and sound can also be stored on a CD disk, making possible MULTIMEDIA applications.

cell an element or block of a SPREADSHEET into which data, numbers or formulae are placed. A cell is created at the intersection of a column and a row.

central processing unit (CPU) the core of a computer system, which contains the INTEGRATED CIRCUITS needed to interpret and execute instructions and perform the basic computer functions. At one time it was used to describe the box that housed the electronics of the computer system. In modern computer systems. It is the integrated circuit that makes use of VLSI (Very Large Scale Integration—up to 100,000 transistors on one chip) to house the control transistors for the computer system.

character a single letter, number, space, special character or symbol that can be made to appear on screen by using the keyboard.

character set the full set of numbers, punctuation marks, alphabetic characters and symbols that a particular computer system uses and that a printer is capable of producing.

characters per inch (cpi) the number of characters that occupy one inch of text when printed. A normal size would be 10 cpi.

characters per second (cps) a measurement of the speed at which a printer can produce type. A DOT MATRIX PRINTER will have a speed of between 120 and 240 cps depending on the quality of print desired.

chat forum a conference area provided by an on-line service provider, such as COMPUSERVE, which allows two or more users to type messages and converse in real time. It is possible to find chat forums on virtually any subject.

check box a small box that is used to TOGGLE between different options in a DIALOG BOX. When the box has a cross or X in it the option is selected; when empty the option is deselected.

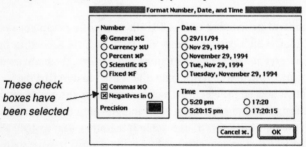

These check boxes have been selected

check sum an error detection technique commonly used in data communications. The sending computer adds the number of bits in a piece of data, sends it along with the data to allow the receiving computer to check that the data is complete. If the check sum is not correct the data is incomplete and an error message is sent.

child *see* GRANDPARENT; PARENT.

chip a tiny chip or wafer of silicon that contains minute electronic circuitry and forms the core of a MICROPROCESSOR or computer. After the initial discovery of semiconductors, technological advance was rapid. Early INTEGRATED CIRCUITS duplicated the functions of a number of electronic components, but now it is possible to create chips that contain unimaginable numbers of components. In fact, it is possible to have 16 million components on a chip smaller than the tip of a finger. Chips can be mass-produced, and after their design, which is undertaken on an enlarged circuit diagram, the circuitry is transferred to plates called photomasks. Using a succession of photomasks, the chip is coated with materials that result in several layers of doped SILICON, and it then forms the equivalent of a highly complex electronic circuit.

chooser a UTILITY PROGRAM for the APPLE MACINTOSH that controls the selection of printers, fax cards and file servers. Once a device is selected, every application can use the device without the necessity for further selections to be set up.

circuit board a plastic board onto which circuits are etched and to which components such as CHIPS and other electronics are connected. The main circuit board for a computer is called the MOTHERBOARD.

circular reference a situation occurring in a SPREADSHEET that is the result of a cell containing a formula that depends on the result of the formula. For example, cell A7 could contain the formula 'sum (a1.a5)' in which the cell a1 contains the formula '=a7'. The addition of a1 to a5 cannot therefore be completed until a7 has a total, and this total will change each time a summation occurs. This process could go on forever in a circular fashion. The user can stop the process by limiting the number of ITERATIONS that can occur.

CISC (Complex Instruction Set Computer) a type of processor CHIP in which an instruction may take several operations and cycles to execute. (*See also* RISC).

clear a command that is used to remove a part of a document. This may be an unwanted paragraph or sentence from a document in a word processing program or a selection of cells from a spreadsheet. Clear commands can usually only be undone until another command is selected. It is important to ensure that you really wanted to clear the selection before you move on to the next command.

click to press and release the MOUSE button. This procedure is done in order to select an item such as an option in a CHECK BOX. The mouse pointer is positioned over the check box, the mouse button is clicked and the check box is selected. (*See also* DOUBLE CLICK).

client a personal computer or workstation in a LOCAL AREA NETWORK that is used to request information from a network's FILE SERVER.

client document a document that is connected to another document (primary) in another computer on a network. When the primary document is updated the client document is updated immediately.

clip art a collection of ready-drawn pieces of art that are available to copy and paste into any document. The purpose is to enhance the look of the document, whether it is a newsletter or promotional flyer. Many graphics packages provide thousands of pieces of clip art.

The signs of the Zodiac are available as clip art. This is the sign of Taurus.

clipboard a temporary storage area into which is placed any selection of a document resulting from a cut and paste or copy and paste command. The clipboard holds the text or graphics after the copy command is issued and until the paste command is issued, at which point the text or graphic is placed into the active document at the selected place.

clock speed a description of the speed of a MICROPROCESSOR usually described in megahertz (one million cycles per second). The system clock emits a stream of electrical pulses or clicks that synchronize all the processor's activities.

clone the original name given to computers that succeeded in replicating the features of an IBM personal computer. Many companies now produce computers that are compatible with the IBM PC but have more features, better components and are built to higher specifications.

close the command to finish working with a computer file. In a GRAPHICAL USER INTERFACE environment, several windows can be open at any one time. Each window has a **close box** that, when checked (*see* CHECK BOX), closes the window.

CMOS (Complementary Metal-Oxide Semiconductor) a chip that features low power consumption.

coaxial cable a cable of the type used for television aerials. It is constructed of an insulated central wire with surrounding mesh enclosed in a plastic cover. The cable type is used in network systems such as ETHERNET.

COBOL (COmmon Business Oriented Language) one of the most commonly used computer programming languages for large mainframe business applications. It has never achieved the popularity of BASIC on smaller computers such as PCs. For large businesses, however, it became the choice for invoicing, salary records and stock control because its programs are easy to read and amend. Its function is to store, retrieve and process such data, and it therefore became useful in automating such processes.

code a list of instructions written to solve a particular problem.

cold boot *see* BOOTSTRAPPING.

cold link *see* LINK.

colour graphics adapter a VDU display standard offering RESOLUTIONS of 640 x 200 pixels in monochrome and 320 x 200 in four colours.

colour monitor a VDU that displays images in multicolours as opposed to a monochrome screen, which is only black and white (or black with green or another colour).

colour separation to print colour commercially, an image has to be separated into its component colours by scanning. The colour scanner directs laser or high intensity light at the image and through filters and a computer converts it into individual pieces of film for each colour used in the printing process. Cyan (blue), magenta (red), yellow and black dots then combine in the four-colour printing process to recreate the chosen image.

column in a SPREADSHEET program a column is a vertical block of CELLS that extends from the top to the bottom of the spreadsheet. The column is usually identified by an alphanumeric character. In a word processing program a column is normally a newspaper style column in which the text flows from the bottom of one column to the top of the next column on the same or succeeding page.

COMDEX the largest computer show in the world. It takes place in the USA twice per year.

comma delimited file a method of saving a file in which each data field is separated by a comma. The comma is a DELIMITER that indicates the end of one field of data and the beginning of the next (or the end of the file). Saving a file in this way makes it easier to transfer files between different programs or computers.

command an instruction or set of instructions that will start or stop an operation in a computer program, e.g. RUN, PRINT, EXIT.

command button a button appearing in dialog boxes that initiates a command such as continue with the operation, cancel the operation or help.

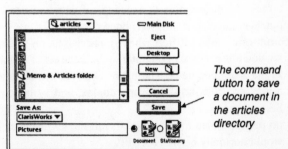

The command button to save a document in the articles directory

command.com an essential command file that is required for DOS to run. The file controls the on-screen prompts, interprets the typed commands and executes the required operations.

command key on a Macintosh keyboard a special key that is used in conjunction with other keys to provide shortcuts for commands. All Macintosh programs use the same command shortcuts.

command line a line of instructions or commands input to the computer through a keyboard. For example, 'format a:' could be typed to tell the computer to format a disk on a: drive.

communications port a PORT at the rear of a computer into which a serial device such as a printer (*see* SERIAL PRINTER) or a MODEM can be plugged.

communications program a program that allows a computer to connect with another computer. This is achieved through a MODEM. Communications programs include telephone directories, facilities that automate the dial-up process, log-on procedures, etc.

communications protocol a list of standards that control the transfer of information or exchange of data between computers connected via the telephone network.

communications settings when you access an on-line service you must set your computer to the same set of standards as the main computer. The main standards are BAUD RATE, PARITY BIT, DATA BITS, STOP BITS duplex, and HANDSHAKING. Settings would be:
no parity; 8 data bits; 1 stop bit; full duplex; handshaking would normally be XON/XOFF.

community the population of an ON-LINE INFORMATION SERV-ICE or BULLETIN BOARD expressing itself in conferences, discussion boards and ELECTRONIC MAIL.

compact disc *see* CD ROM.

compact disc interactive *see* CDI.

Compaq a major manufacturer of IBM-compatible computers. In fact, the computers designed and manufactured by Compaq are of a generally higher quality than most IBM-compatible machines.

compatible a characteristic of word or data processing equipment that permits one machine to accept and process data prepared by another machine, without conversion. This commonly refers to data but also can refer to hardware such as printers, monitors, i.e. IBM-compatible. To be really compatible, it should be possible for a program or PE-RIPHERAL to run on a system with no modification and with everything running as intended.

compiler a program that translates code that has been written in a HIGH-LEVEL PROGRAMMING LANGUAGE into an executable program.

compress to reduce the space taken up by files in order to reduce the disk space that is used to store the compressed files. (*See also* FILE COMPRESSION.)

Compuserve an ON-LINE INFORMATION SERVICE provider that provides a wide variety of services such as ELECTRONIC MAIL, news services, sports results and information, encyclopedia, financial information, computer information, many on-line forums and files to download. The INTERFACE is generally good for GRAPHICAL USER INTERFACE computers, and there is access to the INTERNET.

Compuserve's main options screen

computer an electronic data processing device, capable of accepting data, applying a prescribed set of instructions to the data, and displaying the result in some manner or form. Also any CONFIGURATION of the devices that are interconnected and programmed to operate as a computer system. Typically, this includes a CENTRAL PROCESSING UNIT with keyboard, VDU, printer and some form of disk drive. It also refers to the setting up of a computer system or program to ensure that it matches the needs of the user.

A simple computer system with screen, processor box, mouse and keyboard

computer system *see* SYSTEM.

concatenation the adding of two or more fields or pieces of text together to form one item, commonly used in SPREADSHEET or DATABASE MANAGEMENT PROGRAMS to manipulate data.

concordance file a file that contains a list of words that are to appear in an index. The word processing program uses the concordance file to create the index along with the page numbers that relate to the index words.

condensed type a type style that reduces the width of characters so that more characters are printed per inch of space. Dot matrix printers will print 17 characters per inch in condensed mode.

conditional statement a statement used in computer programming to determine the next operation. Conditional statements are also used in SPREADSHEET and database programming. For example, a salesman's commission can be calculated with a conditional statement such as:

=if(sales>=5000, sales*.10, 400),

which means that if the salesman generates sales greater than £5,000 then a 10 per cent commission is payable, otherwise a flat rate commission of £400 is due. In other words, the result is conditional on the level of sales.

config.sys a DOS file that contains commands that set up the computer's operating system. DOS requires that peripherals and applications have specific start commands that are held in the config.sys file. It is therefore important that the file is not deleted or the various programs or peripherals will not function properly.

configuration the machines that are interconnected and programmed to operate as a computer system. Typically, this includes a CENTRAL PROCESS UNIT with KEYBOARD, VDU, printer and some form of DISK DRIVE. It also refers to the setting up of a computer system or program to ensure that it matches the needs of the user. Configuration has to be performed at the outset, and while modern applications software has automated the procedure to some extent there are certain elements that have to be done manually. Once established, the set-up is saved in a configuration file that should not be erased or altered.

console the terminal that is used to control the computer system. It is applied as a descriptive term to a control device on large MAINFRAME systems. It is also used to describe the KEYBOARD and VDU in PERSONAL COMPUTER systems.

constant a fixed value used in a SPREADSHEET. When using a spreadsheet program, the use of constants has to be carefully monitored. Where possible, constants in repeated formulae should be avoided. One constant in a primary CELL should be used, and all the repeat formulae should be based on the primary cell. If the constant in the primary cell is changed all repeat formulae will automatically change.

context sensitive help an information system incorporated into application programs that automatically finds the relevant pages to assist with a command or operation with which the user is having difficulty. Context sensitive help systems reduce the time that is spent searching through HELP FILES for the appropriate section, thus making the program more user-friendly and allowing the user to be more productive.

control panel a utility program designed to allow the user to alter the look and feel of the computer environment. These utilities control such aspects as screen colours, monitor settings, date and time display, sound and speech settings, mouse controls, etc. (*See also* CDEV.)

Copeland the code name for the next major version of the MACINTOSH operating system.

coprocessor a secondary or support CHIP that is used alongside the main chip to provide added power for specific operations such as graphics display or mathematical calculations.

copy to create a duplicate of a file, graphic or program without changing the original version. Some copy protected programs, however, do not allow an exact copy of an original or key disk to be made.

copy protection a method of preventing, or at least reducing, the user's ability to copy a program illegally. A special code is written into the program that requires that the user type in a PASSWORD or inserts a special disk in order to use the program.

corrupted file a file or part of a file that has become unreadable. Causes of file corruption could include improper handling of a disk, a power surge, flaws on the disk surface or damaged READ/WRITE HEADS.

CP/M (Control Program Monitor) the operating system that dominated the desktop computer world before DOS was introduced in 1981. Control Program Monitor was the trade name used for the operating system for microcomputers based on the Z80 microprocessor chip.

cpi *see* CHARACTERS PER INCH.

cps *see* CHARACTERS PER SECOND.

CPU *see* CENTRAL PROCESSING UNIT.

crash an unexpected termination of an application, usually resulting in the freezing of the computer, i.e. it becomes completely unresponsive. The computer often has to be rebooted to recover (*see* BOOTSTRAPPING).

cropping a feature of graphics programs that allows electronic trimming of a picture either to get rid of unwanted parts of the image or to fit the image into a predefined space.

cursor an indicator on the screen of a VDU, used by a computer to direct a user to the starting position—the point at which data is entered. It can be a small line, a square of light on the screen or an arrow symbol, and can be controlled by use of the mouse or the arrow keys on the numeric pad on the right-hand side of the keyboard.

custom software a computer program that is written specifically for a client to match the systems that the client operates in his or her business. The program is useful only to one client and will probably not be usable by others.

cybernetics a branch of science that is concerned with computer control systems and the relationship between these artificial systems and biological systems.

cyberspace in modern computer communications a user connects with cyberspace when he or she logs on to an online service or connects with another computer. ELECTRONIC MAIL and forum messages move around cyberspace.

D

daisywheel the print wheel for a **daisywheel printer**, which produces LETTER QUALITY printing. It does this by rotating a print element resembling a wheel with spokes. Each spoke contains two characters of the alphabet. Daisywheel printers were once the first choice but have now been overtaken by the technology of printing that has made INKJET, bubble-jet and LASER PRINTERS more readily available.

data jargon for information. Data can be groups of facts, concepts, symbols, numbers, letters, or instructions that can be used to communicate, make decisions, etc.

data bits the elements of a character sent during ASYNCHRONOUS COMMUNICATIONS that contain the actual data.

data bus *see* BUS.

data file a computer file containing data as opposed to an application or program.

data processing the preparing and storing, handling or processing of data through a computer.

database a file of information (data) that is stored on a computer in a structured manner and used by a computer program such as a DATABASE MANAGEMENT SYSTEM. Information is usually subdivided into particular data FIELDS, i.e. a space for a specific item of information.

database management system (or DBMS) a software system for managing the storage, access, updating and maintenance of a database. Users can use it to edit the database, save the data, and extract reports from the database.

daughter board a printed circuit board that plugs into the main board, or MOTHERBOARD, in a computer with the purpose of adding processing power or other facilities.

DBMS *see* DATABASE MANAGEMENT SYSTEM.

debug to locate and correct errors (BUGS) occurring in a application, e.g. when writing the code for a program there will undoubtedly be mistakes made. In order to make the program work correctly the errors must be eliminated. The program must be 'debugged'.

decollator a machine that separates the sheets of a multipart form or continuous paper, i.e. it separates the top sheet from the second sheet.

decryption the process of decoding or deciphering data from an encrypted form (*see* ENCRYPTION) in order that the data can be read and used.

dedicated a term that describes a computer or hardware device that is used solely for one purpose, e.g. when a computer is dedicated to act as a SERVER for a NETWORK.

dedicated line a communications cable line that is dedicated exclusively to a particular communication function. For example, a dedicated line may be used in a building to connect up a number of computers.

default a pre-set preference that is used by a program, the 'fallback' position. For example, in a word processor the defaults for style of type and font may have the default of SANS SERIF 12 BOLD.

delete to erase a character, word, command or program. Once the item is deleted, it may not be possible to recover it, so it is important to be careful about which files, etc, are deleted.

delimiter a character that is used to show the end of a command or the end of a field of data in a data record. Characters commonly used as delimiters are the comma (,), semicolon (;) or tab.

demo (short for **demonstration**) a program that is restricted in some way but still shows a potential user the main features of the program. Usually the features to be disabled are the SAVE and print features. Inevitably, **demo disks** are used to promote and sell software.

demodulation *see* MODEM.

density a measure of the amount of information (in BITS) that can be stored on magnetic media such as a FLOPPY DISK. Single density allows for a measured quantity, but there is also double density. Quad density, or high density, uses very fine-grained magnetic particles, and although they are more expensive to produce than double density, they can store one MEGABYTE or more on a single disk.

descending order *see* ASCENDING ORDER.

desk accessory a small UTILITY program that can help in a computer user's productivity. Desk accessories include items such as notebooks, address books, on-screen calculators and scrapbooks.

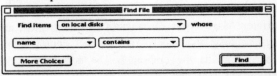

This example of a desk accessory utility program is useful for finding files stored on disk

desktop in an operating system environment that uses a GRAPHICAL USER INTERFACE the desktop is the computer representation of a physical desk top on to which files and folders can be placed.

desktop publishing (DTP) the software and hardware that makes possible the composition of text and graphics as normally done by a printer or in a newspaper office. Desktop publishing requires the use of a computer, LASER printer, and various software programs to prepare and print documents. It is possible to produce anything from a single page of text to advertisements, pamphlets, books and magazines. Computer-aided publishing has been possible since the early 1970s for organizations willing to invest large sums of money, for example, traditional printers or publishing houses. Desktop publishing as a function of PERSONAL COMPUTERS became possible on a broad scale only in 1985, with the introduction of the first relatively inexpensive laser printer producing LETTER QUALITY for type and visuals.

A basic desktop publishing system allows its printer to produce print by employing a variety of FONTS and type sizes, type JUSTIFICATION, hyphenation, and other typesetting capabilities provided by publishing software programs. Page layouts, based on a template, can be set up on the monitor and transferred, as seen on the monitor, to the printer. Many types of GRAPHICS can be created, and the system may also incorporate art and photographs from sources inside the computer. The command codes for producing text and graphics are comparatively simple: some computers use symbols and a pointer controlled by the mouse; others use word and letter commands. A basic desktop publishing system includes a MICROCOMPUTER, a laser printer that is able to print at 300 DOTS PER INCH or more, word processing software, a PAGE DESCRIPTION LANGUAGE, and a software PAGE LAYOUT PROGRAM that enables its user to position, size and manipulate blocks of type and pictures.

In contrast to professionally printed matter, 300 dpi provides relatively LOW RESOLUTION, although greater resolution is now available. More complex laser printers or the use of an added phototypesetting unit produces finer quality print and illustrations. The addition of a computer-connected SCANNER allows the use of text and visual material from other sources.

device driver in DOS a UTILITY PROGRAM that extends the capabilities of the operating system to allow hardware devices such as a mouse, CD ROM drive, printer or hard disk to work with the computer.

diagnostic program a UTILITY PROGRAM designed to test computer hardware and operating systems for errors that may cause or be causing system ERROR MESSAGES.

dialog box a WINDOW that is an integral part of a program and is used to convey information or request information from the user about the operations of the program. A dialog box could have: OPTION buttons, which are 'either/or' buttons; CHECK BOXES, which allow several options from a menu to be selected; LIST BOXES, which present a list of options, one of which can be selected; and COMMAND BUTTONS, which allow the user to continue the operation with the selection or to cancel the operation.

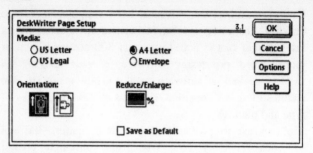

A dialog box concerned with page set-up options

dial-up the process of locating and retrieving information over telephone lines.

digital a term used to describe the use of two states, on or off, in order to represent all data. A computer is digital since it represents all data in a series of 1s and 0s. Using these 1s and 0s, calculations and other operations can be performed in an exact manner.

Digital Research a major manufacturer of computers, including IBM-compatible machines. It was formed in 1957. It also created its own operating system, DR-DOS, similar to MS-DOS.

digitize to convert text, images or sounds into a series of dots that can be read by a computer. It is also the term used to describe the process of scanning (*see* SCANNER).

DIMM (Double Inline Memory Module) a small CIRCUIT BOARD containing RAM chips that increase the amount of memory available to a computer. (*See also* SIMM).

dip switch (Dual In-line Package switch) one of a collection of small 'on' and 'off' switches used to select options on a

CIRCUIT BOARD without having to modify the hardware. They are frequently found inside printers to control vertical spacing and other variable functions and in computers and other electronic devices. A dip switch is the complete unit of plastic that contains the circuit and leads for fitting into the device.

directory the table of contents of a computer file system that allows convenient access to specific files. A directory is an area of the disk that stores files. It is common practice to store the files from one particular application in a specific directory so that they do not get mixed up with other files. Files can then be recognized by their names. When a directory is called up on screen it usually provides several items of information. A name can be given when a disk is formatted and this is the VOLUME LABEL. In addition, the size of files in kilobytes is stated and the directory/file structure is shown.

disk *see* FLOPPY DISK; HARD DISK.

disk cache an area of computer RAM that is used as a temporary storage for frequently used data. It allows faster access to the data than if the data were held on a physical disk. It therefore speeds up processing.

disk drive the piece of hardware and electronics that enables information to be read from, and written to, a disk. The recording and erasing is performed by the READ/WRITE HEAD. The circuitry controlling the drive is called the **disk drive controller**.

dither to combine small dots of different colours or shades to produce the effect of a new colour or shade. For example, the combination of blue dots and yellow dots produces a green image. If the dots of blue are slightly larger than the yellow dots the shade of green becomes darker and moves towards purple. Use of dithering and a palette of 256 colours can produce a continuously variable colour range.

docking station a hardware device into which a NOTEBOOK COMPUTER can be connected to provide added facilities such as DISK DRIVE, CD ROM, colour VDU, PRINTER access, etc. The notebook computer can easily be inserted and extracted from the docking station.

document traditionally, a piece of work created in a word processing program such as a letter, memo or report. Recently the term has been expanded to include work created in a DATABASE MANAGEMENT PROGRAM or SPREADSHEET.

documentation books that provide information and instruction in the use of a piece of hardware or software. Since the books are bulky and expensive to print some manufacturers provide the information on disk. The information can be accessed as a TUTORIAL file or often as part of an ON-LINE HELP system.

document reader a hardware device that scans printed text, converting the text into digital signals. Software can be obtained to convert the digitized files into readable text that can be edited as any word processing document. (*See also* SCANNER.)

DOS (Disk Operating System) the program responsible for communications between a computer and its PERIPHERAL DEVICES such as the DISK DRIVE, PRINTER or the VDU. It controls and manages all the peripheral devices connected to the computer system. It therefore must be the first program to be loaded when the computer is switched on. The commonest OPERATING SYSTEM is MS-DOS (produced by Microsoft Corporation in the USA), which was introduced in 1981.

dot matrix printer a piece of equipment for printing characters. It is an IMPACT PRINTER, and as such is comparatively noisy when compared to the non-impact printers such as INKJET or LASER. A dot matrix image is created by a number of pins striking a ribbon and forming the image on the paper. Printers with just 9 pins produce poor quality output, and although there are versions with more pins, which give better quality, they come second in effect and quality to the newer technologies. They are fast, however, and are still much used for large volumes of repetitive work.

dots per inch (dpi) a measure of the RESOLUTION of a screen or printer. The more dots per inch that the computer can display or print the higher the resolution. (*See also* DOT PITCH).

dot pitch a measure of the RESOLUTION of computer screens or printers. The smaller the dot pitch the sharper the image that is displayed. A dot pitch of 0.28mm is HIGH RESOLUTION while 0.4mm is LOW RESOLUTION.

double-click to click the mouse button twice in quick succession. A control panel utility can be used to set the time delay between clicks of the mouse. A double click can extend the use of the single click. For example, a single click positions the cursor in a word while double clicking selects the whole word. Single clicking on a program icon selects the icon while double clicking will select the icon and open the program. A file can similarly be selected with a double click.

double density disk a FLOPPY DISK that can store approximately 720 kilobytes of data.

double-sided disk a type of FLOPPY DISK with both surfaces available for storage of data. Two READ/WRITE HEADS are required for double-sided disks.

download to copy a file from an ON-LINE INFORMATION SERVICE or from another computer to your computer. It is the opposite of UPLOAD.

down time the time when computer equipment is not available for use because of hardware or software malfunction. This is a very frustrating time since the investment in equipment is not producing results. The selection of reliable equipment is, therefore, important.

dpi *see* DOTS PER INCH.

draft mode the quickest, LOW RESOLUTION output from a DOT MATRIX or INKJET PRINTER. It is used to produce a document used for initial review and editing prior to producing the final full quality output.

drag to hold down the mouse button and move the mouse pointer across the screen. The drag technique is used to select an area of text in a word processor document or to select a group of cells in a spreadsheet or to select a group of document icons in a desk top window.

drag and drop having selected an area of text (for example, in a word processing document) with the drag command, the selection can be dragged from one part of the document to another and then dropped into its new place in the document.

DRAM (Dynamic RAM) a type of computer memory chip that cannot retain memory and so has to be continually refreshed (*see* REFRESH). This type of chip is used to transfer data within the computer.

draw program *see* OBJECT-ORIENTED PROGRAM.

drop down menu a list of command options that appears only when the main command is selected. Use of drop down menus allows programmers to provide many options to the user without cluttering the screen.

drum scanner *see* SCANNER.

DTP *see* DESKTOP PUBLISHING.

dumb terminal a computer terminal that lacks its own CENTRAL PROCESSING UNIT and DISK DRIVES.

dump the process of transferring the contents of memory in one storage device to another storage device or item of hardware. For example, it may be a dump from disk to printer, disk to tape or screen to printer. Dumps are often performed when programmers are debugging programs (*see* DEBUG).

duplex *see* FULL DUPLEX.

DVI (Digital Video Interface) a set of standards or specifications for combining conventional computer techniques with those of video.

Dvorak keyboard an alternative KEYBOARD from the normal QWERTY keyboard. Some 70 per cent of the keystrokes are made on the home row compared with around 30 per cent with the QWERTY layout.

dynamic data exchange an interprocess channel through which correctly prepared programs can exchange data and control other programs.

dynamic link a method of linking data shared by two separate programs. When data is changed by one program it is changed immediately for use by the other. This type of link is required in MULTIUSER networks.

E

echo to show on screen the commands being executed by a computer as they are being performed.

edit to change or alter text, graphics or values that appear in a file. The edit process is required to correct mistakes previously made in a file and is a core function of all word processing software.

edutainment the term given to a growing selection of computer software that educates the user while being entertaining. An example of such a program is Sim City, in which the user becomes the mayor of a town and has to make a variety of decisions that affect its survival and growth.

EGA (Enhanced Graphic Adapter) a colour bit-mapped (*see* BITMAP) VDU display adapter for IBM-compatible PERSONAL COMPUTERS. It displays up to 16 colours simultaneously with a RESOLUTION of 640 x 350 PIXELS.

electronic mail or **email** the use of a NETWORK of computers to send and receive messages. Growth has been restricted in the past because of the variety of incompatible email systems. However, this is being corrected with the INTERNET's standard platform for worldwide electronic mail communications. The use of electronic mail has the advantage over conventional communication of cutting out unnecessary chat and can connect groups of people on a worldwide basis for collaboration on projects.

electronic marketplace every day more businesses are offering their goods and services for sale over the INTERNET. Payment for goods or services in this electronic marketplace is made by credit card and goods are shipped by courier as in normal mail order.

electronic publishing the use of the INTERNET to publish and distribute work. At no time need the work be printed on paper. The type of work that can be the subject of electronic publishing includes on-line news services, on-line encyclopedia or computer-based training manuals.

email *see* ELECTRONIC MAIL.

emulate to duplicate the function of a program, operating system or hardware device in another computer system.

encryption the method of encoding data so that unauthorized users cannot read or otherwise use the data. Data characters can be jumbled by a computer program, communicated to another computer and, as long as the receiving computer has the same encryption program, recompiled into meaningful information.

environment the style or setting in which the user enters commands into or performs tasks with the computer. The GRAPHICAL USER INTERFACES provide an environment or setting that looks similar to a desktop while a DOS system provides a command line environment.

EPROM (Erasable Programmable Read Only Memory) a memory CHIP that can be programmed, erased and reprogrammed.

EPS graphic (Encapsulated PostScript graphic) an object-oriented graphics file format developed by Apple. The format uses separate graphic objects such as lines, rectangles, arcs, ovals, each of which can be independently moved or sized. A file saved in this format can be read by many programs.

erasable storage a READ/WRITE secondary storage device in which data can be written and erased repeatedly. A HARD DISK is such a device whereas a CD ROM is not since it cannot be erased once data is written to it.

erase to rub out or delete from a STORAGE device.

error message a message displayed on a screen that indicates that the computer has detected an error or malfunction. **Error trapping** is the ability of a program to recognize and almost anticipate an error and then carry out a preset course of action in response to the error.

escape key (esc) a nonprinting character or keyboard control key that causes an interruption in the normal program sequence. Within a software program it is usually pressed to cancel a command or operation.

Ethernet a LOCAL AREA NETWORK hardware standard capable of linking up to 1,024 computers in a network. Ethernet can transfer up to 10 megabits per second.

EtherTalk an implementation of the ETHERNET local area network developed by APPLE and the 3com corporation, designed to work with the APPLESHARE network system.

event-driven program a program that is constructed to react to the computer user who initiates events such as clicking a mouse rather than a COMMAND-driven program, which requires specific commands to be typed into the computer to obtain results.

execute to carry out the individual steps called for by the program in a computer.

expansion bus *see* BUS.

expansion card a printed CIRCUIT BOARD that is fitted into the main computer board. Expansion boards are fitted to enhance the power of the computer, providing facilities such as MODEMS, added memory and high speed graphics.

expansion slot a PORT in the main computer system that allows the fitting of an expansion card. There are several slots available for fitting expansion cards in computers.

expert system a program that uses the accumulated expertise in a specific area of many people in order to assist nonexperts who wish to solve problems.

export to create a data file in one program that can be transferred to another computer and be read by another program. Exported files can usually be transferred in a particular format to ensure that they can be read in the new system.

extended memory specification *see* XMS.

F

FAT *see* FILE ALLOCATION TABLE.

fax or **fax machine** or **facsimile** a device capable of transmitting or receiving an exact copy of a page of printed or pictorial matter over telephone lines in, usually, less than 60 seconds. It is currently the preferred method for the rapid transmission of printed material. Facsimile transmission in some form has been available since the end of the last century. The fax was invented by a Scot, Alexander Bain, from Caithness. From the 1920s, newspapers used slow facsimile devices, equipped with photoelectric cells that scanned material placed on rotating drums, to transmit photographs. Police departments, the military and some businesses sent printed matter via matched facsimile machines. However, fax remained a relatively specialized communications device until the development of sophisticated scanning and digitizing techniques in computer and communications technologies and the establishment of standards that made it possible for all fax machines to communicate with one another over ordinary telephone lines.

Most contemporary fax machines conform to a set of standards, known as Group III, that were implemented in 1980 and that require digital image scanning and data compression. Machines built to conform to Group III standards can transmit data at a maximum 9,600 bits per second. To transmit, the original document is fed into the machine, where it is scanned by a mirror-and-lens-aided device, or, in some faxes, by a series of light-emitting diodes (LEDs). Light and dark picture elements—PIXELS—are described digitally, and the message is shortened by compressing much of the white space. The receiving machine, which is addressed through its telephone number, translates the code it receives back into a pattern of greys, black and white. The reconstituted message is printed out on heat-sensitive paper, using techniques similar to those of photocopying machines. Some fax machines can double as copiers, and modern machines use ordinary paper, which eliminates the use of heat-sensitive paper that browns over a period of time.

A standard fax machine

feed the process of supplying paper to a printer. Paper can be fed into the printer either by a friction system or a TRACTOR FEED device, which gives **line feed** when the printer moves the paper forward one line at a time. Laser printers use **page feed**, which ejects one page at a time. (*See also* SHEET FEEDER.)

fibre optics a method of carrying information along cables using light. This method of transmitting data is faster and more reliable than conventional wires. Recent developments have allowed scientists to pass an amount of information equivalent to 1,000 bibles per second along a fibre optic cable.

field a defined group of characters or numbers, e.g. a customer number, a product description, a telephone number or address within a specific space in a DATABASE program.

fifth generation computer the computer of the future. It is the next stage of computer development, which will incorporate technologies such as PARALLEL PROCESSING, SPEECH RECOGNITION, integrated communications, and much more.

file a collection of data that is given a distinct name and is stored on the computer's SECONDARY STORAGE. Files are stored within directories, analogous to the old system of filing cabinet, drawers and folders.

file allocation table (FAT) a table held on a computer disk that keeps a record of the location on a disk of all the files. Files can be distributed in many locations on a disk, and the FAT keeps a record of the locations so that the file appears contiguous, or in one piece, to the user.

file association a link between a document file and the program that created it so that when a document file is selected by double clicking it opens the program and hence the file. Without file association, double clicking the document would have no effect.

file attribute information held in a file directory that contains details about the file and how the computer can access it.

file compression the process of condensing a file with the result that it takes up around half the normal space on a disk. Usually files that are not frequently used, are being archived or are being prepared for electronic transmission are compressed in this way.

file compression utility a program that is designed to COM-PRESS files. There are various programs available that will compress files, e.g. Stuffit, Disk Doubler and JPEG for graphics. (*See also* FILE COMPRESSION).

file conversion utility a program that is designed to convert files created in one program for use by another program. For example, files created in Word can be converted and used by Word Perfect.

file extension *see* FILE NAME.

file format the method that an OPERATING SYSTEM or program uses to store data on a disk. Different software companies have different methods of storing data, with the result that it is difficult for one program to read a file created in another program. (*See also* FILE CONVERSION UTILITY).

File Maker Pro a popular DATABASE MANAGEMENT PROGRAM created by the Claris Corporation. It has versions for both the Macintosh operating system and Microsoft Windows operating system.

file manager a utility program that allows the user to copy, delete, add or move files around without reverting to the DOS commands and to create directories. Microsoft Windows uses a file manager program to assist its users.

file name a name given to a file by the computer user so that the operating system recognizes the file. Every file on a disk directory must have a distinct name. Some operating systems restrict the length of a file name to eight characters that are separated by a full stop from a three character **file extension**. The file extension is often added by default by the program and identifies the file with the software with which it was produced.

file recovery the process of retrieving or restoring a file that has been previously erased.

file server a PERSONAL COMPUTER in a network that provides access to the storage media for workstations or other computers in the network. The operation of the network operating system ensures a seamless view of the server's files from each workstation.

The server is usually a high-powered computer with a very large storage capacity that is set aside as the controller for the clients on the network. (*See also* SERVER.)

file transfer protocol a standard that controls ASYNCHRONOUS COMMUNICATIONS by telephone to ensure error-free transmission of files.

fill an operation that is used in a SPREADSHEET program to enter values in a range of CELLS. For example, a range of dates can be 'filled' into cells to act as headings for a monthly cash flow report.

filter to select certain files from a DATABASE by setting up a set of criteria. For example, to find those records that are dated between 1 and 31 January *and* contain a reference to a particular salesman. An alternative filter would be to find those records containing a reference to a particular salesman *or* referring to a particular customer.

finder a UTILITY PROGRAM that manages memory and files in conjunction with the Macintosh operating system.

firmware the part of the system software that is stored permanently in the computer's read only memory (*see* ROM). Firmware cannot be altered or modified.

fixed disk *see* HARD DISK.

flash memory a type of memory device that can be programmed, erased and reprogrammed. It is retained when the power is turned off. Flash memory cards, similar in size to credit cards, are used to store programs and files for PERSONAL DIGITAL ASSISTANTS, LAPTOP COMPUTERS and NOTEBOOK COMPUTERS where size and space-saving are crucial.

flatbed scanner a hardware device that is used to transfer text and graphics from paper into a digitized format that can then be edited in a computer program. (*See also* OPTICAL CHARACTER RECOGNITION).

A flatbed scanner is similar in looks to a photocopier

flat file database a DATABASE MANAGEMENT PROGRAM that can access only one record or file at a time. This restricts the usefulness of the program compared with a RELATIONAL DATABASE management program.

flicker a distortion that occurs on a VDU, caused by a low rate of refreshment of the screen, i.e. the electron beam does not progress over the screen fast enough to reflect changes in the display when the display is constantly changing.

floating point calculation a form of calculation that the computer employs for calculating numbers. The decimal point in a number is not fixed but floats, allowing a high level of accuracy in calculations. The floating point calculation in some programs can handle numbers up to 10^{20} accurately. Other programs, however, may effectively limit the accuracy of a calculation by reducing the size of the numbers to, say, 10^{15}.

floppy disk a removable secondary medium of storage for computers. The disks are made of a plastic that is coated with a magnetic material (of which the main component is ferric oxide), and the whole thing is protected by a rigid plastic cover (in the case of $3^1/_2$ inch disks). The disk rotates within its cover, and an access hole allows the READ/WRITE HEAD of the disk drive to record and retrieve information. There is a WRITE-PROTECT notch on the disk cover that can be set so that the disk drive cannot change the disk but can only read the data stored there. The $5^1/_4$ inch disks are more susceptible to damage than the $3^1/_2$ inch disks because they do not have a rigid outer cover and are gradually being superseded. However, floppy disks are an essential part of any computing system because they are the means of installing software, backing up files and transferring data between users if no others means exists. The storage capacity of a disk varies and depends upon the size, the density of the magnetic particles coating the disk's surface and the drive used. Some examples are:

size	density	drive	capacity
$3^1/_2$ inch	double	standard	720K
$3^1/_2$ inch	double	standard	800K (on a Mac)

size	density	drive	capacity
3¹/₂ inch	high	high density	1.44M (megabytes)
3¹/₂ inch	high	high density	2.88M
5¹/₄ inch	double	standard	360K
5¹/₄ inch	high	high density	1.2M

A 3¹/₂ inch floppy disk

floptical disk a FLOPPY DISK that, because of its construction, allows the disk drive's READ/WRITE HEADS to align very accurately with the disk. This allows a far greater amount of information to be stored on a disk.

flow when data is being imported into a word processing document or page layout document, the imported text will flow into the available columns and around any graphic images. When one column is filled the text will flow into the next column.

folder in GRAPHICAL USER INTERFACE systems a folder is the DIRECTORY in which files are located or stored. The folder is represented on screen by an ICON styled like a physical folder in a filing cabinet.

font a complete set of letters, numbers, special characters and punctuation marks of a particular size and for one identifiable typeface whether roman or bold (the WEIGHT), italic or upright (the posture). The term is often used to refer to a family of fonts or TYPEFACES, although this is technically in-

correct. Fonts come as bit-mapped (*see* BITMAP) or OUTLINE
FONTS.

font family a set of FONTS sharing the same TYPEFACE but differing in the size and the boldness of the type.

footer text positioned at the foot of a page by a word
processing program, for example. The type of text could
vary from the file name, date, time, page number, origina-
tor or other relevant text.

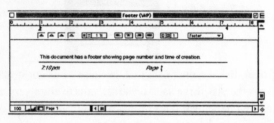

Footer shown on a document

footnote a note at the bottom of a page in a word processing
or page layout document that is used to explain a word or
phrase or concept. The word being footnoted is identified
by the placement of a superscripted number after the word.
This number corresponds to the footnote number.

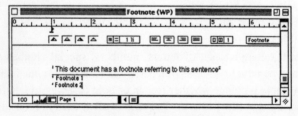

Footnotes shown on a document

footprint a physical measure of the amount of desk space that a computer and its peripheral devices take up when sitting on the user's desk. If the computer footprint takes up the whole desktop space there is no room left to work.

forecasting a method of using past results to project results into the future. For example, future sales can be forecast by analysing the results of past months and years. It is important to look at past years since there may be seasonal trends, such as increasing sales at Christmas, that will have to be taken into account in creating the forecast.

foreground task the priority job that the computer is undertaking in precedence to the other tasks that are being processed in the BACKGROUND. The foreground task is the task that you are monitoring on the computer screen. To support foreground and background processing the computer must be capable of MULTITASKING.

format the preparation of a HARD DISK or FLOPPY DISK for use by laying down clearly defined recording areas (*see also* INITIALIZE). The format is the way in which the magnetic pattern is laid down on the disk.

In particular programs, e.g. a SPREADSHEET, the format is the overall arrangement of labels and values in the separate cells of the spreadsheet. This may relate to the layout of decimal numbers or the alignment of entries within columns. A similar concept applies to DATABASE MANAGEMENT and word processing programs. In the latter the format will encompass all aspects of the typeface, the page layout (numbering, headers and footers) and the paragraph styles.

formatting the process of instruction that produces the desired format of text in a document for on-screen display or printing.

formula a calculation in a program, such as a SPREADSHEET, that defines a relationship between values that can be directly input or are already present in the spreadsheet. For example, a simple task is to add a range of cells with the formula 'sum(a1.a6)'. Or a cell d3 with the value of 66 can be added to the value 24 with a formula 'd3+24', which gives the result 90. There are many functions, such as 'sum', that can be used in a formula, and relatively complex calculations can be carried out automatically. Others include average, cosine, lookup. LOGICAL OPERATORS such as and, or and not can also be incorporated into formulae.

FORTRAN (FORmula TRANslation) a HIGH-LEVEL PROGRAMMING LANGUAGE designed for mathematical, engineering and scientific work. It was developed in the 1950s by IBM.

forum a designated group in which discussion takes place via the electronic network. ON-LINE INFORMATION SERVICE providers set up resources to allow people to choose from a wide range of subjects or to choose a general area where any subject can be discussed (subject to the rules of the service provider). (*See also* CHAT FORUM).

fourth generation computer the current generation of computers that use CHIPS. The use of microchip technology allows computers to be small and lightweight. However, peripheral devices such as power supplies and hard disks restrict how small a computer can be constructed.

fractals groups of shapes that are alike but not identical, such as leaves or snowflakes. No two snowflakes are identical but they have generally similar patterns. Computer programs can create fractals to provide artists and designers with a huge variety of graphic images.

fragmentation the storage of files on a disk that uses noncontiguous sectors to store the file. On a newly formatted disk, a file will be stored in its entirety in one location. The next file to be stored will take up the next sectors, and so on until the disk is full. When several files are deleted the relevant sectors are free for new storage of files, but one sector may not be large enough for a file. The file is therefore fragmented, or split, between two or more available sectors. The process of saving and deleting files will result in a particular file being located in many sectors on the disk. The disk READ/WRITE HEADS will take longer to retrieve the file in such circumstances. Disks can be defragmented using a utility program and thus as much as 50 per cent of the time taken to retrieve a file can be saved.

free form database a form of DATABASE that has no preset structure of information on each record. The information that can be held on one record can be completely different from the information on another record. Such free form databases are useful for storing general notes that are accumulated on a desk notepad, for example.

freeware copyrighted programs that are provided by the author free of charge. These programs, although free, are often troublesome as they may not have been fully tested, resulting in errors or system crashes. More importantly, they may carry a computer VIRUS that could cause complete loss of all files. It is therefore important to use virus detection utilities before running freeware programs.

frequency a measure of the speed at which a computer processor operates. It is measured in MEGAHERTZ.

FST (Flatter Squarer Tube) the technology for producing a VDU or TV screen that is flat rather than having the traditional convex surface.

full backup utility a utility program that creates a full backup of the files on a disk. It is different from an INCREMENTAL BACKUP, which backs up only the files that have been altered since the previous backup.

full duplex a protocol for ASYNCHRONOUS COMMUNICATIONS, which allows the sending and receiving of signals at the same time. Asynchronous communication requires the correct standard of cabling.

function any single operation of a computer or word processor, e.g. editing. Also, within certain programs such as SPREADSHEETS, a procedure that is stored in the program and that will perform a particular sequence of operations or calculations to produce an end result.

function key a special purpose key on the keyboard of a word processor or computer system that enables the user to perform a particular task or execute a command that might otherwise take several keystrokes. Functions differ depend-

These are the function keys on a keyboard

ing on the program. However, there is a general convention to program the keys for the same function, e.g. F1 is used generally to display the help screen.

fuzzy logic a description of the development away from strict logical arguments to take account of human or non-logical behaviour. The development of ARTIFICIAL INTELLIGENCE requires a degree of fuzzy logic since human decisions are rarely based on strict rules of logic.

G

gateway a device that converts communications from one PROTOCOL or BANDWIDTH to another. This function allows two different types of NETWORK to communicate with each other. For example a LOCAL AREA NETWORK (LAN) can communicate with a WIDE AREA NETWORK (WAN), and a LAN can be connected with the INTERNET through an appropriate gateway.

GIF (Graphics Interchange Format) an efficient file compression system for graphic images (pictures). Because of its efficiency, GIF files are used widely for downloading from ON-LINE services.

giga a prefix meaning one billion (a thousand million), and abbreviated g.

gigabyte one billion BYTES or 1,000 MEGABYTES, although, strictly speaking, a gigabyte is 1,073,741,824 bytes. Hard disk capacities of one gigabyte on PERSONAL COMPUTERS are increasingly common.

GIGO (Garbage In, Garbage Out) a common situation where poor or distorted results from a program are caused by incorrect input or mistakes in the input. Thus the quality of the data output is only as good as the quality of the input.

glare the reflection of light from the computer screen. This can be very distracting and can cause stress if not corrected by using a glare filter or by moving the screen.

glitch a malfunction caused by a hardware fault. The malfunction is most often caused by a power surge or interruption.

global a style or format that is applied throughout a document or program. For example, all ruler settings in a word processing document can be set to the same tabs, etc. Similarly, all cells in a SPREADSHEET program can be set to the same numeric format.

glossary in word processing documents a glossary can be used to store phrases or styles that are commonly used. This saves time when keying in text as an abbreviation for the common phrase can be used and then automatically substituted.

goto a programming phrase that directs the program logic to a part of the program in order to accomplish a specific function. Also, a command feature that allows the user to select a page to move to in a word processing document or allows the user to select a cell to go to in a SPREADSHEET program.

grabber a representation of the mouse pointer with which images, text or cells are selected by moving the pointer across the selection required.

grandparent the oldest file in a grandparent, PARENT, son BACKUP system. The grandparent file should not need to be used unless both the parent and child backups have been used and corrupted.

graph a pictorial representation of values that is used to show the relationships between the values. Graphs are an invaluable way of getting a message across. The old adage is 'a picture paints a thousand words'.

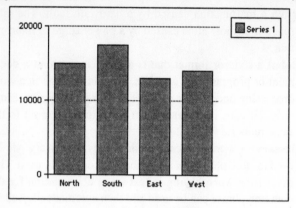

A simple bar chart graph

graphical user interface (GUI) the part of the software program that communicates and interacts with the user by means of pull-down MENUS, DIALOG BOXES and ICONS. The GUI makes computers easier to use because people recognize and respond to graphic representations of concepts, etc, much more readily than if they have to read words. Microsoft Windows utilizes this system.

graphics a generic term used to describe anything to do with pictures as opposed to text. There are two types of graphic images used by computer programs: OBJECT-ORIENTED PROGRAMS or draw programs and bit-mapped (*see* BITMAP) or PAINT PROGRAMS. Object-oriented programs are used where precision graphics are required, e.g. in CAD or architecture programs. Bit-mapped graphics are useful in artistic applications where shading and patterns are more important than precision.

The hand shows a bit-mapped graphic while the line shape is a vector graphic

graphics tablet an input device that uses a touch sensitive pad and a stylus. The movement of the stylus over the tablet generates an electrical pulse that is recorded by the computer and translated into a digital form as a screen PIXEL. The drawing on the pad is thus transferred to the screen.

grey scale the shades of grey from white to black that a computer can display. The more grey scales that are used the more realistic the picture will look. However, memory and storage required increase with the number of grey scales used.

groupware software that is created to increase the productivity of a group of workers in a team using a LOCAL AREA NETWORK.

guest an access privilege in a LOCAL AREA NETWORK that allows an infrequent user to examine certain files on the network without having a PASSWORD.

GUI *see* GRAPHICAL USER INTERFACE.

gutter an additional margin added to a word processing document or page layout document that allows space for a binder without obscuring the text.

H

hacker an individual who is obsessed with finding out more about computers. The term has evolved to refer to people who access other people's computers, usually with the aid of communications technology and without permission. There have been some notable instances of hackers gaining access to top security government systems.

half height drive a DISK DRIVE that occupies approximately 1.6 inches height in a computer drive bay. Originally the drive bay was 3$\frac{1}{2}$ inches high to accommodate the original size of a disk drive. Disk drives have shrunk in size since those early days.

halftone the shading in an image created by use of dots of various sizes and densities. Light areas are represented by small dots spaced apart while dark areas are created by larger dots placed close together. A similar technique can be used to produce flowing colours. Images scanned into a computer can be created in halftones to create usable images for reproduction.

hand-held scanner a scanning device (*see* SCANNER) that can be held in the hand. The scanning head is moved over the text or image to be copied. The image or text is digitized and can be stored in the computer. The image is held as a bit-mapped file (*see* BITMAP) and as such any text in it cannot be edited. However, OPTICAL CHARACTER RECOGNITION

software can be used to translate the text into a usable file
that can be manipulated like any text file.

handle a small black square that surrounds a GRAPHICS image
in an OBJECT ORIENTED PROGRAM, allowing the user to change
the size of the image or to reshape the image or to move the
image around the screen. By choosing the appropriate handle, the image can be changed in one or two dimensions.

handshaking a greeting between two devices, such as a modem to modem or computer to printer, that signals that data
transmission between the devices can proceed. The two
types are **hardware handshaking** and **software handshaking**. In hardware handshaking a control wire is used to
signal when transmission can proceed. In software
handshaking, such as XON/XOFF, a control code is sent to
control the flow of data.

hanging indent in a word processing program this is the format of a paragraph that has the first line starting on the left
margin and the subsequent lines starting further to the right,
as in this text.

hard a term used to describe a hyphen or PAGE BREAK inserted
by the user in a word processing, page layout or spreadsheet program, as opposed to a SOFT command inserted by
the program.

hard card a printed CIRCUIT BOARD (PCB) that plugs into the
EXPANSION SLOT of a computer. The PCB contains a hard
disk drive and controller circuitry. This is an easy way of
adding extra storage capacity to a computer but it is an expensive option.

hard copy a document or file that is printed as opposed to
one that is stored in a computer's memory or stored on disk.

hard disk a fixed disk that forms a storage medium within the computer. It was developed in 1973 by IBM and initially called the Winchester disk, but early versions were very expensive. Today they are a standard component of just about every computer and their mass production has reduced the price enormously. At the same time, the capacity has risen dramatically, from the early sizes of 10, 20 and 40 MEGABYTES to several hundred megabytes and even one GIGABYTE (i.e. one billion or 1,073,741,824 bytes or 1000 megabytes). The hard disk includes the storage medium, the READ/WRITE HEAD and the electronics to connect it to the computer. There are several disks, or platters, that revolve at 3600 rpm, and the head floats just above the disk surface to eliminate wear. The large capacity of hard disks means that several software programs can be installed on one machine plus innumerable data files. Hard disks may fail, however, and it is important to back up data regularly.

hardware interrupt *see* INTERRUPT.

hardware platform the physical equipment of a computer system such as the CENTRAL PROCESSING UNIT, DISK DRIVE(s), VDU and PRINTER. In fact, anything that can be connected to a computer.

Hayes command set a standard set of instructions that have been developed to control communications through MODEMS. Commands include:

AT	attention command prefix	Hn	hang up
A	answer	Ln	speaker volume
D	dial	P	pulse dialling
Fn	select line modulation		

Hayes compatible modem a MODEM that recognizes the

HAYES COMMAND SET, which is the *de facto* standard for ASYNCHRONOUS COMMUNICATIONS between modems.

HDLC (High-level Data Link Control) a PROTOCOL for synchronous communications.

head the device used by a DISK DRIVE to read a disk. As each side of a disk can be read by a separate head the number of heads is often used as shorthand for the number of sides (e.g. double-sided disk).

head crash the physical impact of a disk head on the disk, resulting in damage to its surface and a serious equipment malfunction that usually destroys data stored on the disk. It was relatively common on older systems, but modern high-tolerance engineering ensures that head crashes rarely occur.

header text that is placed at the top of every page in a document. The header normally contains the date, page number and document title. Different word processing programs have a variety of controls over the headers in a document.

heap a part of the computer's memory that is set aside for specific instructions that control such aspects as user input, menus and icons.

help file a file built into a software program that provides assistance and further information about selected topics. The file can be opened while the program continues to run.

hertz (Hz) a measure of the frequency at which electrical waves repeat each second. It is a measurement used to show the speed of a computer CHIP. Generally, the higher the speed of a chip the better is the performance. However, two different chips can operate at the same speed but have different performance levels. For example, an Intel 386 operating at 33 megahertz has lower performance than an Intel 486 operating at the same speed. A computer with a fast PROCESSOR is not necessarily ideal since it depends on the quality of DATA BUS, display (*see* VDU) and DISK DRIVES to determine the performance of a system.

heuristic a method used by experts to solve problems using a rule of thumb rather than strict logic. This is important in developing ARTIFICIAL INTELLIGENCE and knowledge systems.

hexadecimal a numbering system that uses a base of 16. Decimal uses a base of 10 and BINARY uses a base of 2.

Decimal	Hexadecimal	Binary
0	0	0000
1	1	0001
2	2	0010
3	3	0011
4	4	0100
5	5	0101
6	6	0110
7	7	0111
8	8	1000
9	9	1001
10	A	1010
11	B	1011
12	C	1100
13	D	1101
14	E	1110
15	F	1111
16	G	10000

HFS (Hierarchical File System) a disk storage system developed by APPLE to organize files on a HARD DISK. The system allows storage of files in a series of FOLDERS. A folder can be stored in a folder within a folder, etc. A major drawback of this type of filing system is that the user cannot define a path that an application can follow to find a file. Files can be 'lost' within many nested folders and so a FINDER utility is a useful addition to a Macintosh system.

hidden code an invisible code or instruction in a document that controls the appearance of the document when printed. Different codes control styles such as bold type or paragraph indents.

hidden file a file that is rendered invisible because of the way its file attributes have been set. The file cannot be seen in directory listings because it is judged so important that the file should not be altered or deleted.

high density a storage technique for FLOPPY DISKS that can store over 1 megabyte of data on the disk (normally 1.44 megabytes). The disk media must use relatively expensive fine-grained magnetic particles to be capable of storage in high density format.

high-level programming language a set of commands for computers that people can understand. Once the programmer has completed the program, all the commands in the high-level programming language are compiled into their equivalent machine code. The use of high-level languages such as BASIC, C or PASCAL allows the programmer to concentrate on solving the problem rather than on how to tell the computer to perform calculations.

highlight to select an area of a document in order to apply a command to that area or otherwise work with the selection. The selected area is often displayed in REVERSE VIDEO. It is most commonly defined using the mouse by clicking and holding until the desired area is selected.

This is a highlighted portion of text to which a command, such as style in italics, could be applied

high resolution the extra sharpness of the RESOLUTION of high quality PRINTERS and VDUS that produces output with smooth curves and well-defined fonts with no jagged edges. The resolution of a printer or screen is measured in DOTS PER INCH or in the number of PIXELS that can be displayed.

HMA (High Memory Area) an area of 64 KILOBYTES of memory in a DOS system above the first MEGABYTE of memory.

holographic storage a storage technology that uses three-dimensional images created by light patterns projected and stored on photosensitive material. When it becomes available it will store a greater amount of information than CD ROMs.

home computer a computer that is designed or marketed for home use as opposed to office or work use. It is generally perceived as being of lower power or capability than a business computer. However, this distinction is becoming less obvious as the technology advances.

home key a key on a keyboard that has various uses depending on the program being utilized. Normally the home key will move the cursor to the beginning of the current line, current paragraph or current document.

host the computer in a computer NETWORK that provides information, files or programs to other computers or WORKSTATIONS on the network. The host computer can provide information to a LOCAL AREA NETWORK, a WIDE AREA NETWORK or over the INTERNET.

hot key a keyboard key combination shortcut that gives access to a menu command or direct access to a program.

hot link a connection between two distinct documents that automatically copies information from one document (the source) to the other document (the target). Changing the information in the source document will result in a similar change in the target document.

housekeeping activities that are performed to reduce clutter on the computer desktop and disks and generally make for efficient use of the computer. Housekeeping includes deleting unwanted files and programs, reorganizing files into the most appropriate directories, defragmenting disks (*see* FRAGMENTATION), etc.

hypercard an accessory program authored by APPLE. Originally this program was shipped with every Macintosh but it is now supplied commercially.

hypermedia a term used to describe how hypertext concepts can be applied to multimedia.

```
-----  Startup/Resume Scripts:  -------------------------

on startUp
  -- Requires handler: getHomeInfo,checkForMissingFonts
  -- gets and sets the user's preferences
  getHomeInfo
  -- audio Palette startup
  if there is a stack "Audio Help" then -- Δ
    start using stack "Audio Help" -- Δ
    send "startSound" to stack "Audio Help" -- Δ
  end if
  checkForMissingFonts -- inform user of missing fonts
  pass startUp -- so others can use it
end startUp
```

An example of a simple hypertalk script

hypertalk a computer scripting language that is used to

create instructions for HYPERCARD programs. Hypertalk is an event-oriented language (*see* EVENT-DRIVEN PROGRAM).

hypertext the ability to pick up on one word in a document as a route to another area of a document. For example, in a hypertext dictionary a link would exist between a head word and the same word when used in a definition. By clicking on 'document' in this definition the computer would be directed to the definition of 'document'. Such a system is used in the worldwide web to connect pages of related information.

Hz *see* HERTZ.

I

IBM personal computer (IBM PC) a PERSONAL COMPUTER developed by IBM that was released in 1981. Since then the computer technology has developed significantly.

icon a symbol on screen that represents something or some process or function in the computer. Icons are used in a GRAPHICAL USER INTERFACE, and the image of an icon resembles the result of choosing that particular option or command. Programs resident within WINDOWS use numerous icons for tasks such as opening and closing files (which use small pictures of files), printing (a printer), discarding files (a dustbin), and so on. Icons can also represent software programs and enable rapid access to the appropriate program.

System Folder

Examples of two icons representing a folder and a graphic document

IDE interface a type of disk controller that is built into the hard disk drive, cutting out the need for a separate controller or ADAPTER CARD. The drive that connects directly to the MOTHERBOARD is relatively fast and inexpensive.

83

idle time the time during which the computer is turned on but is not processing any instructions. The computer is waiting for a COMMAND.

if a LOGICAL OPERATOR that tests a CONDITIONAL STATEMENT and, if it is true, performs one task; if it is false, it performs another task.

illegal character a character that is not recognized by a command-driven operating system (*see* EVENT-DRIVEN PROGRAM) in a particular situation. For example, in DOS you cannot use an asterisk (*) or a space when naming a file.

image enhancement the improvement of a GRAPHICS image by smoothing out the jagged edges, changing the colours, adjusting the contrast or removing unwanted details.

image processing any process that relates to manipulation of images from the initial digitizing to manipulating the image (embellishing and refining), saving the image and printing the image.

image setter a high quality, professional grade typesetting machine that creates images at RESOLUTIONS of 1200 DOTS PER INCH or more.

impact printer a printer that relies on contact with the paper and an ink ribbon to imprint the character. It is noisy but has the advantage of being able to producing multiple copies of documents

import to open a file that has been created in one application in another application. The file must be in a form that the new application can read it or the new application must have conversion codes available to it.

incremental backup a backup procedure that takes a copy of only the files on a disk that have been updated since the previous backup was taken. FULL BACKUP takes a copy of all files irrespective of when they were last backed up.

index a list of key words created at the end of a document. The index contains the word and the page references where that word can be found. Some word processor and desktop publishing programs create indexes automatically.

index file a file in a DATABASE MANAGEMENT PROGRAM that keeps a list of the location of records using a pointer system. This allows the sorting and searching of a database to be much faster if the whole record is used.

infection the state of having a VIRUS in a computer system. The virus may not be immediately obvious as it can be present on a system for many months before it is activated. This can be caused by a particular series of keystrokes or it may happen on a special date. The activated virus can cause severe problems or can simply display a rude message.

information DATA that has been compiled into a meaningful form. Information is often used interchangeably with data but this is incorrect.

information superhighway the global network of computers connected by satellites and telephone lines. (*See also* INTERNET).

information technology (IT) a jargon term used to describe all computer, telecommunications and related technology that is concerned with the handling or transfer of information. IT is a vast field incorporating the collection, handling, storage and communication of INFORMATION.

init in the Macintosh operating system a UTILITY file that is executed at start-up. It is similar to 'terminate' and 'stay' resident programs in the DOS operating environment. Inits can conflict with each other and cause a system CRASH. Inits include disk drive drivers, fax card drivers, etc.

initialize to start up or set up the basic conditions. When disks or diskettes are initialized, they are formatted to accept data that will be stored later. (*See also* FORMAT.)

inkjet printer a printer type that forms an image by spraying ink on to a page from a matrix of tiny spray jets. Print RESOLUTIONS of 300 DOTS PER INCH are not uncommon with inkjet printers.

input the INFORMATION to be entered into a computer system for subsequent processing.

input device any peripheral device that provides a means of getting data into the computer. The term thus includes the keyboard, mouse, modem, scanner, graphics tablet.

input/output (I/O) the general term for the equipment and system that is used to communicate with a computer. It ensures that program instructions and data readily go into and come out of the CENTRAL PROCESSING UNIT.

insert mode the input mode that allows input to be typed into a document at the CURSOR point. Text already in the document will be moved to allow for the new entries. Overtype mode, on the other hand, deletes previous type as new material is inserted.

insertion point the point at which text can be entered into a document when typing. It is analogous to the CURSOR in old DOS systems.

installation program a UTILITY PROGRAM that is commonly supplied with application software with the purpose of assisting the user to install the software correctly on a hard disk. The utility takes a step by step approach to the installation to ensure that the correct system files are located on the hard disk and to ensure that the various files are located in the correct DIRECTORY or FOLDER.

integrated circuit a module of electronic circuitry that consists of transistors and other electronic components, usually contained on a rigid board. A variety of boards are plugged into a computer to enable it to perform its various tasks.

integrated program a group of software packages each with a logical relationship to the other components. For example, a typical integrated package may include a word processor, a spreadsheet, a database, a graphics application and perhaps a communications application. The common link is that all these applications operate in a similar manner and it is possible to transfer data between them. Major software manufacturers produce many such packages.

integrity the quality associated with a file that is complete and uncorrupted. For various reasons a file can be corrupted. In this case the file is said to have 'lost its integrity'.

Intel a major manufacturing company that makes integrated CHIPS. The range of chips started with the popular 80286 processor and has progressed to the PENTIUM chip.

interactive processing a system in which the user can monitor the computer's processing directly on the computer screen and make any corrections to the process that are required. In the early days of computers, processing relied on BATCH PROCESSING, when the user had to wait hours to obtain the results of the program.

interface the term for the PORTS and the correct electronic CONFIGURATION between two or more devices that help them exchange data. (*See also* USER INTERFACE.)

interlaced a VDU display technology that produces HIGH RESOLUTION pictures but rapidly moving pictures may appear to flicker or streak. Only half the screen is refreshed (*see* REFRESH) on the first pass with the second half of the screen refreshed on the second pass.

internal command a DOS command that is always available at the DOS PROMPT. The COMMAND.COM program is loaded on start-up and contains codes for common internal commands such as copy, dir, prompt and CD (change directory). External commands run separate program files.

internal hard disk a HARD DISK that is located inside the PERSONAL COMPUTER's case. It uses the main computer's power supply and is consequently cheaper than an external hard drive.

internal memory another name given to RAM and ROM, which is where the computer stores information being used by a program or file.

internal modem a MODEM that is located inside the PERSONAL COMPUTER's case and connected directly to the EXPANSION SLOT. It uses the main computer's power supply.

internet a worldwide system of linked computer NETWORKS. The system can link computers that have different operating systems and storage techniques. There is no main source of information or commands as the system was designed to operate even if one network were destroyed.

interpreter a routine that translates a program written in a HIGH-LEVEL PROGRAMMING LANGUAGE into MACHINE LANGUAGE. The interpreter translates each command at a time and then, once the computer has executed the command, it moves to the next line. If an error has been made in the program the

interpreter stops and reports an ERROR MESSAGE. This process allows a novice programmer to learn programming
from his or her mistakes as he or she writes the program.
(*See also* COMPILER.)

interrupt a signal from the microprocessor that temporarily
halts or interrupts processing to allow another operation
such as receipt of input to take place. As soon as the operation has been completed the original process continues. The
computer is constantly faced with such situations. These
are called **hardware interrupts** as opposed to **software interrupts**, which are interrupt signals generated by a computer program.

I/O *see* INPUT/OUPUT.

iteration a COMMAND or program statement that is continually repeated until a particular condition is met. A simple iteration is:

add one to a number until the number is equal to 10.

J

jaggies or **aliasing** the ragged edges that appear on computer GRAPHICS. They are caused by the square edges of PIXELS, which show up when a curve is drawn.

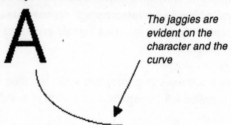

The jaggies are evident on the character and the curve

job an item of work that is performed by a computer, such as BACKGROUND printing of documents.

job queue a series of jobs that a computer is to perform in sequence.

join in a RELATIONAL DATABASE, information from two separate data tables is combined or joined to create another data table that contains summary information.

joystick an INPUT DEVICE controlling the cursor of a computer. The joystick is normally used for controlling computer games.

JPEG (Joint Photographic Experts Group) a FILE COMPRESSION technique that is used to reduce the size of GRAPHICS files by close to 100 per cent. The technique results in some

loss of detail but this is minor in comparison to the size of
the reduced file.

justification the alignment of lines of text in a paragraph
along the margins. Text can be aligned with the left margin,
right margin or both.

Each line of text is shown in a different justification mode

Line one is left justified
                       Line two is centre justified
                                     Line three is right justified

K

K the abbreviation for kilo as in kilometres. It actually means 1000, but in the computer world it is used rather more loosely because 1 KILOBYTE is actually 1024 bytes. It is commonly used to refer to the relative size of a computer's main memory. 64K is equal to approximately 64,000 characters of information.

KB, kbyte *see* KILOBYTE.

kermit an ASYNCHRONOUS COMMUNICATIONS protocol that is used for telephone communications.

kern to reduce or increase the space between two characters in a display font with the result of placing the characters in a pleasing style.

key a button on a keyboard.

keyboard a set of alphabetic, numeric, symbol and control keys that relays the character or command to a computer,

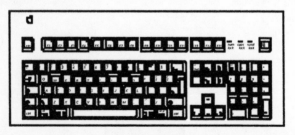

A standard keyboard

which then displays the character on the screen. The keyboard is the most frequently used INPUT DEVICE.

key field the FIELD that is used as the one for sorting data. For example, a SORT of records in a database of customers using the surname of a customer as the key field will provide an alphabetic list of customers.

keypad the same as the numeric keypad, which is the group of numbers at the right-hand side of a keyboard.

keystroke the action of pressing a key on the keyboard resulting in a character being entered or a command being initiated.

keyword a word in a programming language that describes an action or operation that the computer recognizes.

kilobyte (K, KB, kbyte) the basic unit of measurement for computer memory equal to 1,024 BYTES.

knowledge engineering the process of extracting information from experts and expressing this knowledge in a form that an EXPERT SYSTEM can use.

L

label text in a SPREADSHEET program as opposed to a number or formula. A label is used for descriptive purposes such as a heading for a row or column.

LAN *see* LOCAL AREA NETWORK.

language a method of communicating. Humans use languages such as English, Spanish, French, etc, while computers use languages such as C, FORTRAN, BASIC, etc.

landscape orientation an optional way of printing a page of text where the page is turned on its side so that it is wider than it is long. (*See also* PORTRAIT ORIENTATION.)

laptop computer a small portable computer that can operate from its own power supply and can be used almost anywhere. It consists of an integrated LCD screen, keyboard and TRACK-BALL. It is constructed in such a way that it can be carried and operated away from an office base.

Laser-jet a LASER PRINTER manufactured by Hewlett-Packard. Because of its quality and price it has come to be regarded as an industry standard.

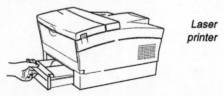

Laser
printer

laser printer a HIGH RESOLUTION printer that uses a technology similar to photocopiers to fuse the text or graphic images to the paper. Output varies from 300 DOTS PER INCH and greater, although 300 and 600 dpi are the commonest resolutions.

launch to start an application or program.

layer an on-screen sheet on which text or graphic images are placed. These images are independent from text or graphics on another sheet or layer. Such layers are used in page layout programs, graphics programs or CAD programs.

layout the process of arranging text or graphics on a page in programs such as word processing or database management systems

LCD (Liquid Crystal Display) a low power display system that uses crystal molecules to display or not, depending on the connection of an electric current. The displays are difficult to read for long periods and are therefore of limited use for computer screens. The use of backlighting makes the screen easier to use but at the expense of using more power.

LED (Light Emitting Diode) a small light used by various computer devices to communicate information about the status of the device.

legend the key on a GRAPH that shows the meaning of the different colours or shades.

letter quality a style of print that matches the quality of impact printing on a typewriter. The LASER PRINTER has replaced the DAISYWHEEL PRINTER as the standard for letter quality printers.

libraries stores of prewritten programming routines for use in generating applications.

light-emitting diode *see* LED.

light pen a stylus used for INPUT, pointed at a computer display that is sensitive to the light from the display.

line art a computer drawing that consists of only black and white areas. There are no shades of grey or halftones. Thus line art can be printed on LOW RESOLUTION printers.

Line art in black and white

line feed *see* FEED.

line graph a style of graph using lines to show the relationship between the variables being plotted.

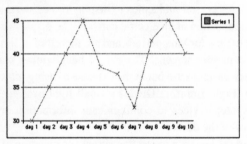

A line graph

line spacing the space between lines of text in a word processing document or page layout program. Most programs allow at least single spacing or double spacing.

link to establish a connection between two computers (as in a NETWORK) or two programs or two files. Where two files are connected the purpose of the connection is to allow the changes in one file to be reflected in the other file. With a cold link the user must initiate a command to update the target file whereas with a HOT LINK the computer performs the task automatically.

liquid crystal display *see* LCD.

LISP (LISt Processing) a HIGH-LEVEL PROGRAMMING LANGUAGE used to a great extent in the development of ARTIFICIAL INTELLIGENCE.

list box a box that appears as part of a DIALOG BOX and lists various options from which the user can make a choice.

load to transfer a program from a computer's secondary storage to the primary memory (RAM) so that it can be activated.

local bus a high speed EXPANSION SLOT that allows high speed transmission of information to travel between the computer processor and a PERIPHERAL DEVICE such as a monitor. The alternative would be to use an expansion BUS, which is slower

local area network (LAN) a grouping of personal computers that are linked by cables within a restricted area. This enables the users to share peripheral devices and information stored either on the individual machines or on a FILE SERVER. The flow of information around the network is controlled by programs using PROTOCOLS or rules. ETHERNET and APPLETALK are examples of protocols.

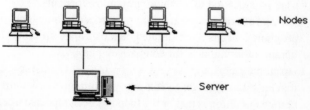

Simple local area network

local drive in a network of computers the WORKSTATION might have a built-in DISK DRIVE, which is referred to as the local drive, as opposed to the server drive or remote drive.

lock to protect a file being altered or changed either accidentally or deliberately. Files can be locked by a software utility or by physically locking a FLOPPY DISK with a WRITE/PROTECT tab.

log off to end a session working at a computer terminal or system.

log on to begin working at a computer terminal or system. In MS-DOS (Microsoft disk operating system) to log on means to activate a drive. In networks, a PASSWORD may be necessary to log on to the system.

logical drive *see* PHYSICAL DRIVE.

logical operator a special word (e.g. AND, OR, NOT) used in a programming statement that expands or limits a search. For example, when searching a database the query may be to find all occurrences of customers living in London. This could be restricted with the revised query find all customers living in London AND who have purchased goods in the last month.

logo a HIGH-LEVEL PROGRAMMING LANGUAGE that is commonly used in education to teach programming concepts.

look-up function in programming, a procedure in which the program consults a pre-defined data list (**look-up table**) to obtain information or for comparison purposes.

loop in programs and MACROS a loop is a set of instructions that tells the computer to continue performing a task until a certain condition is met or the loop has been repeated a certain number of times.

Lotus a major software design company that made its first major impact with the SPREADSHEET package Lotus 123.

lowercase *see* UPPERCASE.

low-level programming language a style of computer language that uses codes or expressions that are similar to the MACHINE CODE instructions understood by the processor chip. (*See also* HIGH-LEVEL PROGRAMMING LANGUAGE.)

low resolution screen or printer output that is of low quality. The fewer DOTS PER INCH that a printer can produce, the lower the quality. The fewer PIXELS on a screen the lower the quality of output. Lower resolution produces more JAGGIES on an image.

luggable a PERSONAL COMPUTER that is too big to be described as portable but is small enough to be transported easily from place to place.

M

machine code the basic 1s and 0s a computer processor uses as its instructions.

machine language a BINARY language that all computers must use. Machine code uses the lowest form of coding, binary, to instruct the machine to change the numbers in memory locations. All other computer languages must be compiled from their high-level code into machine code before the programs can be executed.

Macintosh a line of computers designed and manufactured by Apple Computer. First released in 1984, they introduced GRAPHICAL USER INTERFACE to the PERSONAL COMPUTER world.

Mac OS the version of the disk operating system written by APPLE that is packaged with their MACINTOSH computers.

macro a record of commands used regularly in an application that can be activated by a keystroke. The macro could be a list of commands used to print a report. Without the macro, the report will require several commands to be executed while if they are recorded in a macro, one command or keystroke can be initiated to print the report.

magnetic disk a secondary storage device that consists of a plastic disk coated with magnetically sensitive material. Magnetic disks are usually described as floppy disks or hard disks depending on their construction. Hard disks generally have a higher storage capacity.

magnetic field a force surrounding electrical devices that can have an adverse effect on data stored on MAGNETIC MEDIA.

magnetic media any of a wide variety of disks or tapes, coated or impregnated with magnetic material, on which information can be recorded and stored. The magnetic coating is repositioned when influenced by a MAGNETIC FIELD, and the READ/WRITE HEAD emits a magnetic field when writing to the disk or tape, which produces a positive or negative charge corresponding to that item of data. When reading, the head senses the charges and decodes them. Disks are used universally but for very high capacity storage, magnetic TAPE is ideal.

magnetic tape *see* TAPE.

mail gateway an electronic path that allows ELECTRONIC MAIL to be sent between different mail services or direct to a computer on the INTERNET.

mailbox within the ELECTRONIC MAIL system, a disk file or memory area in which messages for a particular destination (or person) are placed. Modern BULLETIN BOARD communications systems use a mailbox metaphor to store messages for electronic mail users. The bulletin board system is a telecommunications utility that facilitates informal communication between computer users.

mail merge the process of merging two files for the purpose of creating a mail shot. One file consists of a letter while the second file consists of a database of names and addresses. Each name and address in the database is merged with the letter, creating a letter addressed to each name in the database.

mainframe any large computer such as an IBM or a Cray. They do not use the same architecture as small desktop computers and are intended for use by many people, usually within a large organization. To begin with, it referred to the large cabinet that held the CENTRAL PROCESSING UNIT and then to the large computers, developed in the 1960s, that could accommodate hundreds of DUMB TERMINALS. Now the word mainframe applies to a computing system that serves the needs of a whole organization.

main memory *see* RAM.

margin the space between the edge of a page and the start of the text.

math coprocessor a chip used for performing FLOATING POINT CALCULATIONS.

MB, mbyte *see* MEGABYTE.

megabyte (MB, mbyte) one million bytes (characters) of information. The common storage measurement for memory and hard disks, e.g. 4 megabytes of RAM, with a 210-megabyte HARD DISK drive.

megahertz (MHz) a measurement of one million HERTZ.

megastream a name used by British Telecom for its high speed digital communication lines.

membrane keyboard a style of keyboard covered by a touch sensitive material to prevent liquid or dirt entering the keyboard circuits.

memory the circuitry and devices that are capable of storing data as well as programs. Memory must be installed in all modern computer systems. It is the computer's primary storage area, e.g. RAM as distinguished from the SECONDARY STORAGE of disks. Typical memory devices are SIMMS, which are plugged into the MOTHERBOARD of the computer. SIMMS are plug-in modules that contain all the necessary chips to add more RAM to a computer. The motherboard is the large circuit board that contains the CENTRAL PROCESSING UNIT, RAM, EXPANSION SLOTS and other microprocessors.

memory address a code or name that refers to a specific location where data is stored in a computer's RAM.

memory cache *see* CACHE.

memory management the process of efficiently using a computer's memory. Most OPERATING SYSTEMS have built-in memory management systems to control the use of memory and its allocation between conflicting programs.

memory map a map that shows how the OPERATING SYSTEM utilizes the RAM.

memory resident program a program that remains in memory ready for use at any time. The program occupies a proportion of the RAM.

menu a list of commands or options that are available to the computer user on a monitor or VDU. A user is presented with a menu that will give a choice of commands or applications. Menus make the computer system easier to use. A PULL DOWN MENU is a selection of commands that appears after a command on the MENU BAR of a program has been selected. A command or action is selected and often another menu will appear. The term originated from an idea by MACINTOSH. Menu-driven software contains programs that proceed to the next step only when the user responds to a menu prompt.

menu bar the area of a screen that is given over to the listing of menu items.

File **Edit** Format Arrange Options View

A menu bar

menu-driven program a program that proceeds to the next step only when the user responds to a menu prompt.

merge to draw two pieces of information or records together to create a new file or for a particular purpose, such as merging a letter file in a word processor with a data record in a database to create a mailshot.

microchip *see* CHIP; MICROPROCESSOR.

microcomputer a small computer, traditionally the smallest size of computer, which is desktop size. The modern use of the term includes any small computer system. In many ways the term has lost its relevance, and its meaning has been somewhat blurred by technological developments. Initially it referred to any computer that had certain key units on one INTEGRATED CIRCUIT called the MICROPROCESSOR. The first PERSONAL COMPUTERS, designed for single users, were called microcomputers because their CENTRAL PROCESSING UNITS were microprocessors. However the distinction between a microcomputer and a minicomputer has all but disappeared, and many microcomputers are now more powerful than the MAINFRAMES of a few years ago.

microfloppy a $3^1/2$ inch FLOPPY DISK. It is encased in a plastic shell to protect it from superficial damage.

microprocessor or **microchip** an electronic device (INTEGRATED CIRCUIT) that has been programmed to follow a set of logic-driven rules. It is essentially the heart of any computer system. Also, a processor that is contained on one chip.

microsecond (µs) one millionth of a second.

millisecond (ms) one thousandth of a second.

Microsoft the world's largest software company. Microsoft has developed numerous items of software including oper-

ating systems (DOS, Windows, and OS/2) and applications
programs (Excel, Word).

MIDI (Musical Instrument Digital Interface) a set of standards that can be used to connect musical instruments, such
as digital pianos, to computers.

migrate to move from using one computer platform to another or from one software application to another. A user
can migrate from Windows to OS/2 operating systems.

minicomputer a computer system, usually smaller than a
mainframe but larger than a microcomputer, designed for
many users.

mini tower a small tower style computer system designed to
sit on a desk rather than the floor where a normal tower system would sit.

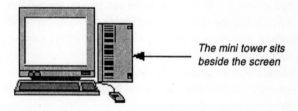

*The mini tower sits
beside the screen*

MIS (Management Information Systems) the current name
given to the subject of data processing.

MISC (Minimum Instruction Set Chip) the basis of the next
generation of computer chips. They take the concept of RISC
chips one stage further.

MNP (Microcom Network Protocol) a STANDARD developed
by the communications company Microcom. It is primarily
aimed at error detection and correction between communications devices.

mode the state of operation of a computer. In COMMAND mode, the computer will accept commands, in INSERT MODE, text can be inserted into an existing sentence, in EDIT mode text can be amended. A computer responds in different ways depending on the mode.

mode indicator a message displayed on screen that indicates the MODE of operation in which the computer is set, such as EDIT mode, INSERT MODE, sleep mode, wait mode, etc).

modem (MOdulator/DEModulator) a device for converting a computer's DIGITAL signals into ANALOGUE signals that can be transmitted down a telephone line. The modem is an extremely important device, enabling communication and transfer of data all over the world. In order that modems facilitate communication between computers, the modems at each end of the line must conform to the same PROTOCOL.

module part of a program or set of programs capable of functioning on its own.

moiré a type of graphic distortion seen as flickering on the screen caused by placing several high contrast line patterns too close to one another.

monitor another name for display, screen or VDU.

monochrome a type of monitor that displays only black and white pixels (or black with green or another colour).

monospace a font type that uses an equal amount of space for each character in the font family:

`'Courier is a monospaced font.'`

'Courier is a monospaced font.'

The difference between a monospaced font and a proportionally spaced font can be seen in the above text.

morphing a technique that appears to melt one image into another image to create a special effect, such as creating the impression that a person changes into a panther. The effect is created by filling in the blanks between the figures so that the change from one figure to another is gradual.

motherboard the main printed circuit board in a computer. It contains the main processor chips, the display controllers, sound chips, etc.

Motorola a major manufacturer of processor chips, such as the Power PC range, which rival Intel's PENTIUM processor range.

mouse an input device that controls the on-screen CURSOR. Movement of the mouse on the desktop causes a similar movement of the cursor around the computer screen.

A mouse

MS-DOS Microsoft's disk operating system.

MTBF (Mean Time Between Failures) a measure of the reliability of a computer or, more particularly, of the reliability of a component used in the manufacture of the computer.

multimedia the process of combining computer data, sound and video images to create an environment similar to television. The market for multimedia on compact disks is now expanding rapidly.

multisync monitor a COLOUR MONITOR that automatically adjusts to the input frequency of the adapter card that is used by the computer (VGA, super VGA, etc).

multitasking where a computer processor can undertake more than one task or operation at a time. For example, a print job can be processed at the same time as a spreadsheet is calculating. Compare with BACKGROUND operations.

multithreading the procedure used to describe when a program splits itself into separate tasks or threads. Each thread can operate concurrently with the others.

multiuser system a system that allows more than one user to operate the system at any one time.

multiplexing a technique that is used in LOCAL AREA NETWORKS to allow several signals to pass along the cables at one time. In this way several computers can access the network simultaneously. Special multiplexing devices must be incorporated, which mix the frequency of the signals being sent along the network. The presence of these devices increases the cost of the network.

N

nano a prefix representing one billionth.

nanosecond (ns) one billionth of a second. These units of measure are used to indicate the speed of operation of a computer CHIP.

nanotechnology the study of how to make computers smaller and more efficient. The term also covers the science associated with the effect of making materials and components smaller.

native file format the format in which a particular program saves a file. The file is saved with certain key characters or codes that tell the program about the various display options associated with the file. The native file format refers to the coding style used by the particular program. Different programs have different formats but can often use the formats for another program to assist FILE TRANSFER.

natural language a language such as English, French, etc, as opposed to an artificial language such as BASIC or COBOL.

near letter quality a mode of operation for DOT MATRIX PRINTERS that produces characters at typewriter quality. This mode has become outdated because of the advent of LASER PRINTERS and INKJET PRINTERS, which produce high quality output faster and quieter.

Netware the Novell company's operating system for LOCAL AREA NETWORKS.

network the interconnection of a number of terminals or computer systems by data communication lines. It may consist of two or more computers that can communicate between each other. Networks for PERSONAL COMPUTERS differ according to scope and size. LOCAL AREA NETWORKS (LANs) usually connect just a few computers (although it may be more than 50), perhaps in order that they can share the use of an expensive PERIPHERAL DEVICE. Large systems are called WIDE AREA NETWORKS and use telephone lines or similar media to link computers together. In general LANs cover distances of a few miles, and some of the largest versions are found in universities and large companies. Each user has a WORKSTATION capable of processing data, unlike the DUMB TERMINALS of a MULTIUSER system.

network administrator the individual who is in charge of a LOCAL AREA NETWORK assisting users and ensuring the correct software is used.

network interface card an adapter card that allows networking cable to be connected directly to the computer. MACINTOSH computers have a basic networking system built into the computer.

network operating system the operating system that is used as a controller for all network components. The network operating system controls FILE SERVER software, the individual workstation software and the network hardware.

network server *see* FILE SERVER; SERVER.

news group a group of people who use an on-line service to discuss interactively topics of mutual interest.

neXT a computer workstation designed by Steve Jobs who was a founding member of APPLE COMPUTER. The computer uses the UNIX operating system with a GRAPHIC USER INTERFACE.

nickel cadmium battery or **NiCad battery** a type of rechargeable battery used in NOTEBOOK and LAPTOP COMPUTERS.

nickel metal hydride battery a rechargeable battery that is more powerful than the NICKEL CADMIUM BATTERY and so is more suitable for NOTEBOOK and LAPTOP COMPUTERS.

node a connection point that joins two devices, such as the joining of a WORKSTATION to a NETWORK. The workstation is commonly referred to as a node of the network.

noise static that is caused by electrical interference and that can reduce the effectiveness of data communications. DIGITAL communication lines do not suffer interference in the way that ANALOGUE lines do.

non-impact printer a PRINTER that produces text output on plain or special paper without contact between the printing mechanism and the paper. Typical examples are INKJET, bubblejet or LASER PRINTERS. Most are capable of high quality print.

Norton utilities a suite of UTILITY programs from Symantec Corporation, which include undelete options, performance testing programs, and so on.

NOT *see* LOGICAL OPERATOR.

notebook computer a small computer that is generally more compact than a LAPTOP. These are useful for mobile users but are not very satisfactory for sustained usage.

Novell a corporation that specializes in software solutions for networks.

null modem cable a cable used to connect two computers without using a MODEM. These cables are generally used to transfer files from a mobile computer, such as a notebook, to a desktop machine at an office to ensure that files are consistent between the computers.

numeric format in a SPREADSHEET, the way a number can be displayed is controlled by use of the numeric format command. The number can be displayed in a variety of ways, including with no decimals; with two decimals; with currency prefix; as a date or time.

numeric keypad a section of the keyboard that allows numbers to be entered in an easy format (*see* KEYPAD).

num lock key a keyboard key that when pressed fixes the keypad to NUMERIC FORMAT rather than the optional controls or characters.

O

object linking and embedding (OLE) a set of STANDARDS designed to allow links to be created between documents and applications, thereby enabling information in one document to be automatically updated when the information in the other is changed.

object oriented graphics graphics that are created by a program that creates an image by a mixture of lines, rectangles, ovals, etc, which can be moved independently. Object oriented graphics can be resized without distorting the image.

object oriented programming system a programming environment that consists of a range of objects that have their own programming code. The objects are incorporated into a program by combining them in the sequences required. A drawback with object oriented programming is that it operates slowly and uses a large amount of memory. It is, however, an easy way to be introduced to programming.

OCR *see* OPTICAL CHARACTER RECOGNITION.

OEM (Original Equipment Manufacturer) a business that makes a piece of hardware as opposed to the company that buys the hardware, reconfigures it, relabels it and sells it to the end user. There may be only a few OEMs in the industry that make laser printer drivers but there may be many companies selling laser printers, many of which will have different features.

off-line equipment that is not under the direct control of the CENTRAL PROCESSING UNIT. A printer may be in an off-line state when it is switched on but not capable of receiving data from the computer.

offset similar to GUTTER, it is the space added to a left margin to allow for the document binding.

off the shelf software a software application that is mass-marketed and serves a general purpose, rather than CUSTOM SOFTWARE, which is developed for a specific customer. (*See also* PACKAGED SOFTWARE.)

OLE *see* OBJECT LINKING AND EMBEDDING.

on-line the operation of terminals and peripherals in direct communication with (and under the control of) the CENTRAL PROCESSING UNIT of a computer, i.e. switched on and ready to receive data.

on-line help a utility associated with a particular application that provides a help system for reference while the application is being operated.

on-line information service a profit-making organization, such as America On-line or COMPUSERVE, that makes information available to its members or subscribers via telephone services. The on-line providers also provide CHAT FORUMS and libraries of information on a vast range of subjects.

open to access a file with its associated application in order to edit the file or print a hard copy of it.

open bus system a design of the MOTHERBOARD where the expansion BUS has slots into which EXPANSION BOARDS can be fixed.

operating environment *see* ENVIRONMENT.

operating system a suite of computer programs (systems software) that control the overall operation of a computer. Operating systems perform the housekeeping tasks such as controlling the input and output between the computer and the PERIPHERAL DEVICES, and accepting information from the keyboard or other INPUT DEVICES. Common operating systems are MS-DOS (*see* DOS), OS/2, UNIX, XENIX. OS/2 (Operating System/2) was developed ultimately by IBM although initially it was a joint development with Microsoft. However, when Microsoft devoted its energies to the improvement of WINDOWS, IBM took OS/2 and it has now gained more acceptance although it is nowhere near rivalling the market share of Microsoft Windows. UNIX is written in language C and was developed by AT & T Bell Laboratories in the 1970s. It can be used on computers from PERSONAL COMPUTERS to MAINFRAMES, and it is suited to MULTIUSER systems. XENIX was produced by Microsoft for use on IBM-compatible computers.

optical character recognition (OCR) an information processing technology that can convert readable text into computer data. A SCANNER is used to import the image into the computer, and the OCR software converts the image into text. No single software package provides a foolproof conversion of text, but the more sophisticated ones have various means of highlighting queries and even recognizing certain unclear characters once the user has responded to the first case. It is a useful tool for inputting large amounts of typewritten or already printed text for editing and changing.

optical disk a type of disk that uses light to write data to the disk and read the data from the disk. It can hold large amounts of information but has slower access times than other SECONDARY STORAGE such as hard disks. CD ROMS use optical disk technology

optical fibre a glass filament that is used to transmit data. Optical fibres can carry huge amounts of information over long distances and do not suffer from electrical interference as do conventional copper wires.

optical mouse an input device that is connected to a computer by light beams rather than wires. This allows the mouse more freedom on the user's desk.

option a choice that the user faces when operating a computer. The simplest options appear in DIALOG BOXES where the choice of command is large but may be print, cancel, options or print preview.

OR *see* FORMULA; LOGICAL OPERATOR.

orientation type can be laid down on a page in a vertical format (PORTRAIT ORIENTATION) or in a horizontal format (LANDSCAPE ORIENTATION). Portrait orientation shows the page taller than it is wide and landscape orientation shows the page wider than it is tall.

OS/2 an operating system created by IBM, which brought a GRAPHICAL USER INTERFACE environment to the the PERSONAL COMPUTER along with MULTITASKING and other advanced features.

outline font a font for printer and screen in which each character is generated from a mathematical formula. This produces a very much smoother outline to a character than can be obtained from a bitmapped font (*see* BITMAP). The use of mathematical formulae means that characters can be changed in size quite easily and only one font need reside in the memory. (*See also* TRUETYPE).

outline utility a UTILITY PROGRAM that is often incorporated in word processing programs and that allows the user to organize thoughts and concepts before creating a report.

output most computer output comes in the form of printed reports, letters and other printed data, or information sent to a mass storage device such as a hard disk drive or a tape drive. The most common output form, however, is the image on the screen. Output devices are peripherals, such as a printer, a magnetic tape drive or floppy disk, that will accept information from the computer.

output device any device that produces a usable form of output from the computer. Printers produce a hard copy of files, documents, etc. A fax machine produces output to another fax machine. A screen (VDU) lets the user view output and a sound card allows the user to monitor sound output.

overtype mode *see* INSERT MODE.

overwrite to save a file on to a disk under a file name that already exists. The original file is deleted—overwritten by the new version.

P

pack to COMPRESS a file. It means saving files in a way that utilizes a minimum of disk space.

packaged software software that is mass-produced, marketed and sold. The software is the same for all users, unlike CUSTOM SOFTWARE, which is written specifically for a client. (*See also* OFF THE SHELF SOFTWARE).

page break a mark in a document that indicates the end of one page and the start of the next. A page break can be generated in a document by use of a menu or embedded command. The page break is extensively used in word processing or spreadsheet programs to provide the presentation required.

It is possible to differentiate between page breaks. **Soft page breaks** are placed automatically by a program, and as text is inserted, the page breaks move automatically. **Hard page breaks** are inserted into a document by the user and retain their position relative to the existing text.

page description language (PDL) a programming language that tells a printer how to print out a page of text or graphics. Any application that can generate output in a PDL can drive any printer, thus making it device-independent. In order that the printer can interpret the PDL it requires its own processor and memory.

page feed *see* FEED.

page layout program an application that allows the user to mix text and graphics in a document of virtually any page size and almost unlimited extent. Both text and graphics can be inserted from other software programs. DESKTOP PUBLISHING is made possible by page layout programs such as PAGEMAKER and Quark XPress.

PageMaker a leading market PAGE LAYOUT PROGRAM published by the Aldus Corporation (now Adobe). One of the pioneers of DESKTOP PUBLISHING, it is highly flexible and permits the incorporation of text and graphics into a document, achieving electronically what hitherto was accomplished by the typesetter and designer.

page preview a feature of many programs that shows the user the way a full page will appear in print. Page preview can show exactly the format to be printed and will also allow checking of margins, headers and footers along with the placement of graphics.

pages per minute (ppm) a measurement of the number of pages that a printer can output per minute.

pagination the process of dividing a document into pages and numbering the pages ready for printing.

paint program an application that allows the user to create pictures or drawings on the computer by selecting the individual PIXELS that make up the screen display. Paint programs have progressed since the first versions of programs, like Macpaint for the Apple MACINTOSH and Paintbrush for DOS.

palette the menu of colours, brush styles or patterns that can be chosen to create an image in GRAPHICS programs.

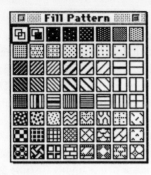

A palette of shading options

pane a term used for each section of a SPLIT SCREEN window. In SPREADSHEET programs a window can be split into four separate panes to make moving around it easier.

Pantone a system that allocates numbers to a range of colours in order that the exact colour match is made. The system is used by graphics studios and print shops to ensure that the colour used in the printing is the colour that the artist or designer requires.

paperless office an office in which paper is no longer used or generated. The term was coined some years ago when computers became commonplace, but in practical terms the computer revolution has tended to produce more paper rather than less. However, as technology advances with electronic mail, scanners, fax cards, etc, the era of the truly paperless office may be approaching.

parallel columns a feature of word processing or page layout programs that sets two or more columns side by side.

parallel communication *see* SERIAL COMMUNICATION.

parallel port a port or slot on the back of a computer that is used to transmit high speed SYNCHRONOUS data streams. It is an extension of a computer's internal DATA BUS and is used primarily for connection to printers.

parallel printer a printer designed to be connected to a PAR-ALLEL PORT. The printer cable connection should not be more than three metres long as the risk of interference increases with the length of the cable.

parallel processing the use of two processors combined to undertake one task. The technique is used where there is a requirement for a massive number of calculations, such as in predicting the weather or high quality graphic processing. Parallel processing should be compared with MULTI-TASKING, which is the use of one processor to undertake two or more tasks simultaneously.

parameter a step in any program sequence that will cause the program to take a specific course of action. It is a value that is added to a command to ensure the task is undertaken in the desired manner. For example, to format the disk in drive A one would type FORMAT A: and the A: is the parameter of the FORMAT command.

parent file in a series of three BACKUPS of a file the parent file is the second oldest file. A conventional backup procedure is to keep three copies of important files. The first is the child, the next the parent and the oldest is the GRANDPARENT.

parity bit an extra BIT added to transmitted data that allows checking for communications errors. The parity bit is attached to each BYTE of data and indicates whether the sum of the bits is odd or even. When the receiving MODEM receives the data, a check is performed to ensure that the sum of the bits (odd or even) is the same as the parity bit. If not, an ERROR MESSAGE is reported.

park to remove the READ/WRITE HEAD from a hard disk to an area of the disk that contains no data in order to protect files during transportation of the disk. If during transport the read/write head touches the surface of the disk there is the risk of data loss. The procedure to park the read/write heads can be achieved automatically or by using a **park utility** program each time the computer is to be moved.

partition a section of a HARD DISK that is created for a particular purpose. A hard disk can be divided, or partitioned, into several parts. For example, one partition could hold the main OPERATING SYSTEM, a second could hold an alternative operating system such as UNIX. A third and fourth could contain data files relating to each operating system. The hard disk can also be partitioned for security purposes, with a PASSWORD required to access the different partitions.

Pascal a HIGH-LEVEL COMPUTER PROGRAMMING LANGUAGE. It has waned in popularity with the advent of C. It was originally designed by Niklaus Wirth for the teaching of structured programming. It is very popular in colleges and schools, and is used as a teaching language and in the development of applications. It is similar to BASIC in that the computer is told what to do by statements in the program. It has some disadvantages in that it is too slow for large-scale development, and commercial versions are changed sufficiently to make them individually isolated.

passive matrix display a form of LCD screen display used for LAPTOP and NOTEBOOK COMPUTERS. A transistor is used to control an entire row or column of the display's electrodes. This type of display is cheap to produce and uses lower battery power than the more expensive but higher quality AC-

TIVE MATRIX DISPLAY, which uses a single transistor for each display electrode.

password a key word that is selected by a user to protect files from unauthorized access.

password protection a means of allowing files to be protected from unauthorized use. The password may be set up in such a way as to protect the file at different levels. For example, entry of the password could allow the user to read the file but not to edit it, or to have full access to edit and copy the file.

A filemaker document requiring a password before access

paste a part of a 'cut and paste' procedure in text editing by which a selection of text from a document is moved to or copied to a CLIPBOARD. Once the text is on the clipboard it can be pasted or moved back to a selected area of the document.

path the means of pointing to the exact location of a file on a computer disk. It uses a hierarchical structure of directories (*see* DIRECTORY) in which files are stored. It is the name given to the location of the file, using the directory structure. For example, a file called THISYEAR stored on the C drive in a directory called ACCOUNTS, has the path C:\ACCOUNTS \THISYEAR.

PC (Personal Computer) a MICROCOMPUTER that can be programmed to perform a variety of tasks for home and office. PCs can be equipped with all the necessary software and other devices to perform any task. They can be part of a large DATABASE or a small NETWORK. The boundary between the PC and former specific computing set-ups such as WORKSTATIONS and MINICOMPUTERS is now blurred. Workstations are powerful computers for use by designers, architects and engineers and feature computer-aided design (*see* CAD) software. PCs are now evolving to this level of sophistication, and similarly are in many instances performing the functions asked of a minicomputer. In colloquial use, PC is used to refer to IBM-compatible computers, i.e. those running DOS or WINDOWS operating systems as opposed to UNIX or MAC OS.

PCB *see* HARD CARD.

PC card *see* PCMCIA.

PC DOS the version of the disk operating system written by Microsoft Corporation that is packaged by IBM with their personal computers.

PCI (Peripheral Component Interconnect) a STANDARD created by INTEL dealing with the process of communicating directly between PERIPHERAL DEVICES and the computer processor. This standard supports PLUG AND PLAY, whereby the peripheral device can be connected to the computer and immediately used without further setting of DIP SWITCHES.

PCMCIA (Personal Computer Memory Card International Association) a group of manufacturers that has set a STANDARD for credit card-sized PERIPHERAL DEVICES such as memory cards, fax modems, sound cards, etc. The devices are designed primarily for NOTEBOOK COMPUTERS. The credit card-sized expansion cards originally referred to as PCMCIA cards are now more commonly referred to as PC cards.

PDA *see* PERSONAL DIGITAL ASSISTANT.

PDL *see* PAGE DESCRIPTION LANGUAGE.

peer to peer a style of LOCAL AREA NETWORK where all the computers are connected to one another and have access to all the information in the network rather than having a central computer that is used solely as a FILE SERVER containing the files accessible by the network users.

pen computer a style of computer that can recognize handwriting as a method of input. The computer has a touch-sensitive screen onto which the user writes with a pen-like device called a STYLUS. The computer interprets the writing and converts it to a digital form as if the input had been typed. Handwriting recognition software is constantly improving but still requires that the input writing is in the form of print rather than cursive writing.

pentium the name of the latest microprocessor chip from INTEL. The pentium is a RISC that contains over three million transistors. It can operate at speeds of more than double that of it predecessor, the 486DX2 chip. (S*ee also* POWER PC.)

peripheral device a generic term for equipment that is connected to the computer. These are external (to the CENTRAL PROCESSING UNIT) and include such devices as external DISK DRIVES, PRINTERS, MODEMS, CD ROMS, SCANNERS and VDUS.

personal computer *see* PC.

personal digital assistant (PDA) a portable battery powered computer, slightly larger than the palm of a hand, which is generally used for a small range of specific purposes such as note taking, address book, agenda calendar and to do lists. Some PDAs, such as the Newton, have handwriting recognition systems, and most have the facility to use a fax, modem and PC card.

personal information manager a DATABASE MANAGEMENT PROGRAM designed specifically to emulate a diary, address book and notebook. These are best used with a NOTEBOOK COMPUTER or PERSONAL DIGITAL ASSISTANT, since a diary or notebook held on a desktop computer is not very useful while the user is away from the desk.

physical drive the hardware that is used as the storage device for a computer. A computer can have more than one physical drive. This can be compared with a logical drive, which could be a partition of a physical drive or a section of the RAM set aside to act as a storage area.

pica a measure of FONT size equal to 12 POINTS ($^1/_6$ of an inch).

PICT (abbreviation for picture) an object oriented graphics file format developed by Apple for the MacDraw program. The format uses separate GRAPHICS objects such as lines, rectangles, arcs and ovals, each of which can be independently moved or sized. A file saved in this format can be read by many programs.

pie graph a form of graph used to present data in a visually attractive fashion. Pie charts are generally shaped like a circle and may have offset or exploded sections to highlight a particular figure.

PIF (Program Information File) a file containing information about DOS applications that assists Microsoft WINDOWS in running the application. The file contains data such as the filename, how to display the file and the amount of memory to use. Windows can run a DOS application even if there is no PIF available.

pin feed similar to TRACTOR FEED.

piracy the unauthorized copying of software, the rights of which belong to someone else. This is theft. (*See also* SOFTWARE PIRACY).

pitch a measurement of the number of characters that a printer prints in a linear inch. Pica pitch uses 10 characters per inch while elite pitch uses 12 characters per inch.

pixel a picture element that is the smallest dot that can be displayed on a screen. The pixels make up the picture to be displayed on screen.

plasma display a type of display screen that uses charged gas particles to illuminates the screen.

platen part of the friction device that pulls paper through a printer. The platen also acts a solid surface on to which the write head can impress the image onto the paper.

platform independent the description of a NETWORK that allows computers using different operating systems to be present. For example, a network of Macintosh computers can have one or more PCs on the network, and vice versa.

plot to create an image using lines rather than a series of dots.

plotter a hardware device that creates drawings by moving a series of pens, usually of different colours, across a page. Plotters are commonly used in computer-aided design (*see* CAD) applications and other detailed graphic presentations.

plug and play a technology that allows a PERIPHERAL DEVICE to be connected to a computer and then used without further setting of DIP SWITCHES. The computer will automatically create the necessary connections. This technology was advertised in the WINDOWS 95 operating system and has been used in MACINTOSH computers since 1985.

point the size of a FONT generated by a printer. There are 72 points in an inch. Normal fonts are printed at around 10 points. It also refers to the use of the mouse or other pointing device, such as a TRACKBALL, to position the CURSOR at a specific place on the screen. Additionally, it is to point to commands or data located in a separate record in a DATABASE MANAGEMENT PROGRAM.

point and click a description of the process of using a device that POINTS, such as a MOUSE or TRACKBALL, to select a command. The user points to a menu command or file and clicks the mouse or trackball button once or twice and the command is selected or the file is opened.

pop up menu a menu of command options that appears on the screen when the user points and clicks a particular part of the screen or uses a second mouse button. (*See also* PULL DOWN MENU).

port a plug or socket through which data may be passed into and out of a computer. Typically, each input and output device requires its own separate port. Most computers have a PARALLEL and a SERIAL PORT. The parallel port is a high-speed connection to printers while the serial port enables communication between the computer and serial printers, modems and other computers. In addition to receiving and transmitting data, the serial port also guards against data loss.

portable computer a computer that can be packed up and

moved to a different location. Some so-called portable computers would be better described as LUGGABLE. Truly portable machines weigh less than 10 pounds, can be contained in one case and have their own battery power. (*See also* NOTEBOOK COMPUTER).

portrait orientation a description of the normal way of printing a page of text. The page is longer than it is wide. (An A4 page is 297 x 210mm (11$\frac{1}{2}$ x 8$\frac{1}{4}$ inches).

POST (Power On Self Test) a test that a computer carries out on start-up to ensure that the main components are working correctly.

post to add data to a record in a DATABASE MANAGEMENT PROGRAM or similar program, e.g. for keeping accounting records.

Postscript an example of a PAGE DESCRIPTION LANGUAGE for printing, created by Adobe. It is the most popular PDL in use because it is regarded as an industry standard.

power down to turn off a computer. It is important to power down correctly as most programs must be shut down in a proper sequence otherwise data may be lost or corrupted.

power PC a MICROPROCESSOR chip manufactured by Motorola and used by IBM and APPLE. It uses RISC technology and has the advantages of being relatively cheap to manufacture and consuming less power than other chips. (*See also* PENTIUM).

power supply a device in a computer that converts the AC mains supply to DC current used by a computer. The power supply tends to be heavy and contributes greatly to the weight of a computer.

power up to switch on a computer and load the OPERATING SYSTEM ready for use.

power user a computer user who is able to use all the advanced features of a program or series of programs. A power user would be generally regarded as an expert.

ppm *see* PAGES PER MINUTE.

precedence the order in which arithmetic operations are performed. The order is important when creating formulae, e.g. in a computer program or spreadsheet. The rules of precedence are (1) exponential equations; (2) multiplication and division; (3) addition and subtraction. For example, the formula 6+5+9+8/4 does not give the average of the four numbers since the division is carried out before the additions. The result of the above is 22. In order to obtain the average of the four numbers, the formula must force the additions to be performed first. This is done with brackets as follows (6+5+9+8)/4, giving the correct average of 7.

primary document *see* CLIENT DOCUMENT.

primary storage a computer's main RAM or ROM, unlike SECONDARY STORAGE such as hard disks, compact disks and optical disks.

printer the device that produces hard copy. Two main technologies are used: IMPACT PRINTERS, which operate by striking an ink ribbon onto paper to produce an image; and NONIMPACT PRINTERS, which make no contact with the paper. Printers vary enormously in quality of output, speed, fonts available, and so on. In addition to the DAISYWHEEL and DOT MATRIX PRINTER, which are impact printers and have distinct disadvantages in terms of flexibility and quality, there are the non-impact printers. The INKJET PRINTER creates text and graphics by spraying ink on to the page, and there is always some risk of smudging the image. Although their RESOLU-

TION and quality does not approach that of the LASER PRINTER, however, they do tend to be less expensive. Laser printers use a process similar to that of photocopiers whereby ink powder is fused on to the paper. To begin with, the major disadvantage of laser printers was their high cost, but with the advent of reasonably priced machines, the benefit of high quality print, quiet running and built-in fonts is more widely available. There are other types of printer available, e.g. THERMAL, but they do not form a significant part of the market.

printer font a FONT that a printer keeps in memory and uses to produce output on a page. The printer fonts sometimes differ from the display fonts used on screen, but with TRUE-TYPE and POSTSCRIPT, the display fonts are the same as the printer fonts.

printer port a port or slot on the computer to which a printer is connected. The port may be a SERIAL or a PARALLEL PORT.

print queue a list of files to be printed that are temporarily held by a PRINT SPOOLER. The print spooler operating in the BACKGROUND sends each file in turn to the printer while the computer can operate normally in the FOREGROUND.

print spooler a UTILITY PROGRAM that maintains a queue of files waiting to be printed. The print spooler sends a file to the printer whenever the printer is ready to receive another document.

processor a device in computing that can perform arithmetical and logical operations.

processing the normal operation of the computer acting upon the input data according to the instructions of the program in use.

Prodigy an ON-LINE INFORMATION SERVICE providing on-line shopping, news reports, CHAT FORUMS, ELECTRONIC MAIL, etc. It was developed by IBM and Sears.

program a set of instructions arranged for directing a digital computer to perform a desired operation or operations. Programmers use a variety of HIGH-LEVEL PROGRAMMING LANGUAGES such as BASIC, C and FORTRAN to create programs (*see* PROGRAM LANGUAGE). At some stage the program is converted to MACHINE LANGUAGE so that the computer can carry out the instructions. Computer programs fall into one of three categories:

(1) system programs, which are the programs required for the computer to function. They include the OPERATING SYSTEM (e.g. Microsoft disk operating system, MS-DOS).

(2) UTILITY PROGRAMS, which includes those programs that help keep the computer system functioning properly, providing facilities for checking disks, etc.

(3) APPLICATION PROGRAMS, the programs that most people use on their computers, such as word processing, database management, financial packages, desktop publishing, graphics and many more.

programmable something is programmable if it is capable of receiving instructions to perform a specific task. A computer is programmable since you can instruct, or program it, to perform a variety of tasks.

programming the procedure involved in writing instructions that the computer will follow to perform a specific task. Programming is part art and part science. The process can be summarized as follows:

(1) decide on the purpose of the application.

(2) collect and write down all the important factors and variables, using flow charts to depict the decision processes.

(3) translate the ideas into a programming language.

(4) compile the program to convert it into machine language that is understood by the computer.

(5) test and eliminate errors from the program.

(6) over a period of time make adjustments to enhance the program.

programming language a language that is used by computer programmers to write computer routines, e.g. COBOL, BASIC, FORTRAN, PASCAL, C, Visual Basic. The HIGH-LEVEL PROGRAMMING LANGUAGES, such as BASIC, C, Pascal, are so called because the programmer can use words and arrangements of words that resemble human language, and this leaves the programmer free to concentrate on the program without having to think of how the computer will actually carry out the instructions. The language's COMPILER OR INTERPRETER (both programs the former of which is the faster) then turns the programmer's instructions into MACHINE LANGUAGE that the computer can follow.

prompt a symbol or message that informs the user that the computer is ready to accept data or input of some form. A prompt could be 'Are you sure you want to quit the program?' Yes or No. A more common prompt in DOS is C:>, which tells you that the computer is waiting for input.

proportional sizing the process by which the user changes the size of a GRAPHICS object without altering the relative dimensions of the image.

proportional spacing a font in which each letter takes up space relative to the size of that letter. For example, the letter m takes up more space than the letter i. This compares with a MONOSPACE font, which allocates the same space to each letter.

proprietary a term for technology that is developed and owned by a person or company who restricts the use of the technology. If anyone wants to use that technology a fee or licence has to be negotiated. Some developers, on the other hand, make their technology open or available to anyone who has a use for the technology. APPLE uses proprietary systems for its MACINTOSH, and IBM restricts the use of the code in its ROM.

protocol the conventions or rules that govern how and when messages are exchanged in a communications network or between two or more devices. There are many different protocols, but communicating devices must use the same protocols in order to exchange data.

public domain software a computer program that the author has decided to distribute free to users. Others can then re-distribute the software without any permission being required. The author may put restrictions on the use of the program, but most SHAREWARE is not advanced enough to re-strict code use.

pull down menu a selection of sub-options related to a command name on the main menu bar. For example, a style command on the main menu bar could have the sub-options of bold, italic, underline, double underline, superscript, subscript, text colour.

Q

quad spin CD ROM a CD ROM that spins at a rate four times faster than the original CD ROM drives. Information can be accessed the more quickly the faster the CD ROM spins.

query in a DATABASE MANAGEMENT PROGRAM, a query is when the user asks the program to find a particular reference or type of data that is in the records of the database.

queue when two or more files are waiting for an action to take place. For example, in a LOCAL AREA NETWORK several users may send files to the printer for output. Each print job is added to a queue and is processed in turn.

Quickdraw the OBJECT-ORIENTED graphics and text display technology that is coded into the ROM of MACINTOSH computers. It is used for drawing GRAPHICS on screens and printers.

quit to exit from a program. It is important to quit from a program in a proper fashion, i.e. through the correct menu command, as failure to do this could result in loss of data or program preferences.

QWERTY the standard typewriter/computer keyboard, denoted by the letters on the top line of characters. It was originally developed to slow down typists to stop the manual typewriters jamming the keys. There are now other alternatives to QWERTY keyboards that enable faster use and easier learning. One such system is the DVORAK KEY-

BOARD, which places the most frequently used letters together.

Key layout on a QWERTY keyboard

R

radio button a round button that allows the user to choose one of a range of OPTIONS in a DIALOG BOX. Option buttons differ from CHECK BOXES in that several options can be checked in check boxes but only one radio button option can be chosen.

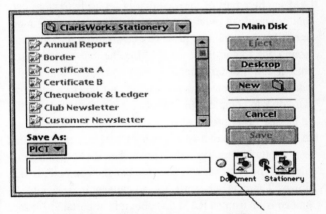

Radio buttons to select document or stationery

RAM (Random Access Memory) or **main memory** or **internal memory** the memory that can be, and is, altered in normal computer operations. The RAM stores program instructions and data to make them available to the CENTRAL PROCESSING UNIT (CPU), and the CPU can write and read data. Application programs use a part of the RAM as a temporary place of storage, allowing modification of the file in use until it is ready for storage permanently on disk. Any work in the RAM that has not been saved will be lost if the power fails.

random access the retrieval of information randomly from any part of the computer memory or from magnetic media, which means that the computer can reach the information straight away without having to go through a series of locations to reach the desired point.

random access memory *see* RAM.

RAM cache a part of the RAM that is set aside to store data and programs in order that the computer can operate more speedily. The computer processor can transfer data and program code to and from the RAM cache many times faster than it can transfer data and program code to and from a hard disk. If the CENTRAL PROCESSING UNIT had to wait on the hard disk to complete an operation there would be no point in having faster processors.

RAM disk an area of RAM set aside by a UTILITY PROGRAM that is formatted to act like a disk drive. The RAM disk is volatile, and the contents will be lost when the computer is shut down. There is a significant advantage in speed to be gained from using a RAM disk, but it is important to ensure that data is stored onto a floppy or hard disk on a regular basis to avoid the risk of data loss.

range a CELL or a group of contiguous cells in a SPREADSHEET program. A range of cells could include a ROW, part of a row, a COLUMN, a part of a column or a group of cells spanning several rows and columns. Ranges are usually given names that relate to the information contained in the range. For example, the range D5.. D9 might contain sales for a division of a business and could be given the name 'salesdiv1'. Any future reference in a formula to the range D5.. D9 could use 'salesdiv1', e.g. Sum(salesdivl).

raster display the type of display found in TV sets. An electron beam scans the screen many times a second, moving in a zigzag pattern down the screen. Each horizontal line is made up of dots that are lit up individually to create a pattern

reboot to restart the computer without turning off the power. The computer's primary RAM memory is initialized and the operating system is reloaded. (*See also* BOOTSTRAPPING.)

read to retrieve information stored on magnetic media and transfer it to the memory of the computer.

read.me file a text file that is often included with program disks and contains up-to-date information about the program, provides updates to the program's instruction manual or gives technical hints or tips about the operation of the program.

read only attribute information stored in a file's directory that tells the computer whether or not the file can be modified or deleted. If the file is read only, it cannot be changed in any way.

read only memory *see* ROM.

read/write head the electromechanical means whereby information stored on magnetic media can be retrieved and transferred to the memory of the computer.

read/write head alignment a DISK DRIVE must be correctly set up otherwise it may not be able to read a disk correctly.

Incorrect alignment may be caused by jolting the computer during transport.

real time the near-instantaneous processing of data and feedback so that the user can respond immediately to the computer program. Programs that use real time processing include flight simulator games, on-line chat forums and point-of-sale recording.

recalculation method the selected method chosen to recalculate a SPREADSHEET after the values in a CELL or number of cells have been changed. The spreadsheet can be automatically recalculated or it can be manually recalculated when the user commands.

recalculation order the sequence that a SPREADSHEET program uses to calculate a spreadsheet. When spreadsheets first appeared, the method of recalculation was restricted to COLUMN-wise or ROW-wise, i.e. the calculation proceeded down one column before moving to the next column. This produced some errors if the spreadsheet logic was not well thought out. More recent spreadsheets use a natural recalculation method that scans the sheet to find the logical recalculation order and calculates a CELL only once all dependent cells have been calculated.

record to store data on a disk. Also, all the information related to a topic in a database of information. For example, in a database of customers of a business a record will contain all the relevant information about one customer

recover to restore lost or damaged files. The files can be recovered by restoring from a BACKUP copy or undeleting the file. The backup may not have the most recent changes recorded, and so the full, up-to-date information may not be

recovered. The undelete method depends on the information on the disk not having been overwritten. UTILITY PRO-
GRAMS that undelete files are commercially available.

redlining the process of marking changes or additions to the
text of a document when comparing different versions.

---

the circuitry and devices that are capable of storing data
as well as programs. Memory must be installed in all
<u>modepn</u> computer systems. It is the computer's primary
storage area, e.g. RAM (random access memory) as distinguished from the secondary storage of disks. <u>Tipical</u>
memory devices are SIMMs, Single In-line Memory Modules, which are plugged into the motherboard of the computer.

Errors are highlighted ready for editing

reformat to repeat a FORMATTING operation on a disk or to
proceed with a formatting operation on a disk that has already been formatted. In word processing, page layout or
spreadsheet program, to reformat means to change the arrangement or style of the text.

refresh to update the image on the computer screen. The
screen is being constantly updated by an electron gun firing
electrons at the phosphorous screen. When the computer
processor sends a change to the video output it must be reflected on the screen. Each time the screen is refreshed it
will reflect the changes.

refresh rate the speed at which the monitor updates its display.

relational database a type of DATABASE MANAGEMENT PRO-
GRAM in which data is stored in two-dimensional tables that

are indexed for cross-reference. Reports can be created using data from two files that are related in a particular way, such as by customer name. For example, one file could contain information on a customer's name and address and another could contain details about stocks of goods. A report can be created showing the amount of one type of stock bought by a particular customer.

relational operator a sign that is used to specify the relationship between values. Relational operators are used in queries on databases. For example, to obtain a report on transactions between two dates an expression such as

$$=>'1/12/95' \& =<'31/12/95'$$

will extract a list of transactions between 1 and 31 December 1995. Other relational operators are:

=	equal to
<	less than
>	greater than
<=	less than or equal to
>=	greater than or equal to
<>	not equal to

relative cell reference a reference to a CELL in a SPREADSHEET that refers to its position with regard to another cell rather than an absolute reference.

release number the decimal number that is used to identify an improvement in a version of a software program.

removable storage any SECONDARY STORAGE system where the storage medium can be extracted and taken away from the computer. Magnetic tapes, floppy disks and disk cartridges are examples of removable storage.

rename to change the name of a file, directory or disk.

repaginate documents are divided into pages for reporting purposes and when text is added to a page the division between the pages is changed. For the user to see where PAGE BREAKS occur, the document must be repaginated. Some programs repaginate the document automatically.

repeat rate the rate at which a character will be typed on the screen when a particular key is kept depressed.

report a presentation of information in print. The report will be complete with page numbers, footers and headers. It will be formatted in such a way as to make it attractive and easy to read.

reset button a button on a computer (often on the front panel) that allows the user to perform a WARM BOOT or restart of the computer. It does not switch the computer off. (*See also* BOOTSTRAPPING.)

resolution a measurement of the sharpness of an image generated by a printer or VDU. Printer resolution is measured in DOTS PER INCH. The more dots per inch, the greater the sharpness of the image on the paper. VDU resolution is measured in the number of PIXELS and their size. The smaller the pixel and the more there are on screen, the greater the resolution of the image. (*See also* DESKTOP PUBLISHING, DOT PITCH, HIGH RESOLUTION, LOW RESOLUTION).

restore to recreate the conditions or state of a disk, file or program before an error or event occurred to destroy or corrupt the data. Restoration would normally involve use of a BACKUP file made previously.

retrieve to obtain data previously stored on file in order that work can be done on the data.

return a COMMAND KEY on the keyboard that is used to initiate a chosen command.

reverse video a state in monochrome monitors in which instead of black text on a white background displays white text on a black background.

> **WHAT DO I PAY FOR YOUR SERVICE?**
> Our current charges for undertaking the preparation of the necessary claims and submitting these to the Inland Revenue is £150 inclusive of VAT, which is payable on completion of the accounts.

The text is in reverse video

rich text format a STANDARD relating to the creation of a TEXT FILE in a way that the FORMATTING details are available to other programs. Use of the standard allows files to be transported between applications, possibly by telephonic communication, without loss of the format of the text.

right justification the alignment of text in a word processing document along the right margin of the document.

Right justified text, such as this, often looks odd.

ring back systems a security system for communications over telephone lines. When the system answers a call from a remote computer system, it confirms the identity of the remote computer and returns the call using a pre-stored telephone number. Unauthorized access to the main computer is therefore restricted and only authorized users can communicate in this way.

RISC (Reduced Instruction Set Chip) a chip that has a limited number of instructions that the processor can execute, thus increasing the speed of the PROCESSOR. The processor is designed to emphasize the most common instructions and to allow these instructions to work as fast as possible.

robot an electromechanical device that may perform programmed tasks. Robots are commonly used in automated factories to perform repetitive functions. The first industrial robots were developed in the early 1960s, although they consisted of little more than an automated hand. Japan subsequently invested heavily in robots and other countries have now followed suit. Primary uses include welding, painting and component assembly.

A common idea of a robot

ROM (Read Only Memory) the part of a computer's internal memory that can be read but not altered. It contains the essential programs (system programs) that neither the computer nor the user can alter or erase. The instructions that enable the computer to start up come from the ROM, although the tendency now is to put more of the operating system on ROM chips, rather than putting it on disk.

root directory in DOS, the top level or first directory on a disk in which subdirectories are created.

row in a SPREADSHEET program a row is a horizontal block of CELLS that extends from the left to the right of the spreadsheet. The row is usually identified by an alphanumeric character.

ruler in a word processing environment, a bar at the top of the page to assist the user in setting margins and tab stops.

run to initiate or execute a program. The computer reads the code from the disk and stores all or part of the code in the RAM. The computer can then perform tasks.

run time version a special version of an INTERPRETER that allows one application only to be run. For example, a program may have been written in PASCAL and will require a Pascal interpreter. However, the user may not have a Pascal interpreter in his or her computer system. The solution is that the program has its own limited or special interpreter that will only work only with that program.

S

sans serif a plain type style or FONT, such as Helvetica, that has no detail at the end of the main character stroke.

This is sans serif text

This is serif text

save to transfer the contents of a computer's RAM to a less volatile memory such as a HARD DISK or FLOPPY DISK. It is recommended that work is saved at regular intervals otherwise there is the risk of losing work if the RAM memory is deleted. This can happen if there is a power supply failure or a system CRASH.

scalable font a FONT that can be reduced or enlarged to any size required without distorting the font shape. Postscript and TRUETYPE fonts are examples of scalable fonts.

scaling in presentation graphs, the y-axis can be scaled to produce a GRAPH that displays the data in a more visually pleasing form or in a way that emphasizes the results being depicted on the graph.

scanner a piece of hardware that copies an image or page into a computer by creating a DIGITAL image. A scanner works by bouncing a beam of light off the paper and recording the reflected light as a series of dots similar to the original image. If the dots are created as a variation of 16 grey values, the scanner is using a tagged image file format (*see* TIFF), otherwise a dithered image is created (*see* DITH-

ERING). This is a simulation of a HALFTONE image, which is created by varying the size of, and the space between, the dots to create the image. Digital halftones become distorted when they are sized. Scanners are available in three basic types: a drum scanner, a FLATBED SCANNER or a HAND-HELD SCANNER.

scrapbook a UTILITY PROGRAM that can be used to retain frequently used images, pictures or text. Company letterheads, logos or party invitations are among the items that can be stored permanently in the scrapbook file.

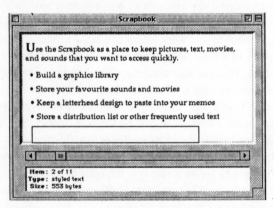

A scrapbook

screen another name for the VDU, display or monitor.

screen capture to take a 'snapshot' of the screen at a particular moment. The snapshot can then be used to explain an entry in a technical manual or dictionary of terms.

screen dump a printed output of a snapshot of the screen.

screen font a FONT that is used by a program to display text.

ADOBE TYPE MANAGER and TRUETYPE fonts produce screen
fonts that are SCALABLE and produce exactly the same design in printed output.

screen saver a UTILITY PROGRAM that is designed to prolong
the life of a screen. Over time, images burn into the screen,
causing a ghost image or reduced sharpness. The screen
saver utility prolongs the life of the screen by switching off
the image after a period of non-use. Alternative screen sav-
ers create moving images on the screen, such as stars,
bouncing balls, fish, flying toasters, etc.

script a list of instructions that automatically perform a task
within an application program. The script is a program
within a program but can easily be written by automatically
recording a series of keystrokes. For example, a user manually enters the commands, telephone numbers and pass-
words to allow entry to an on-line information service.
Once the user is logged on, the keystrokes to retrieve certain information are recorded. The final sequence to log off
is also recorded. The next time that the information is to be
retrieved from the on-line service the script can be selected
to control the process automatically.

scroll to move the ACTIVE WINDOW over a document so that a
different part of the document is visible in the window.
Scrolling can be vertical or horizontal. In a word processing document scrolling vertically allows sight of the various pages in the document. Horizontal scrolling allows
sight of a horizontally oriented spreadsheet.

SCSI (pronounced 'scuzzi', Small Computer System Interface) an INTERFACE connection that allows high speed transfer of information between a computer and one or more pe-

ripherals such as hard disks, scanners, or printers. The devices can be connected in a chain so that one SCSI port can support several devices at a time, although data can only be transferred from one device at a time.

second generation the era in computing technology that is represented by use of transistors rather than vacuum tubes in computing devices. This generation was evident in the early 1960s and was superseded by the THIRD GENERATION, when INTEGRATED CIRCUITS replaced the transistor.

secondary storage or **auxiliary storage** a form of permanent storage of data on disk drives. The drives can be HARD DISKS, magnetic tapes, FLOPPY DISKS, CD ROMs or OPTICAL DISKS. The main feature of secondary storage is that it is not deleted when the computer's power is turned off.

sector a storage area on a disk. When a disk is formatted it is organized into TRACKS and sectors. A sector is a pie-shaped division of the magnetic surface on the disk that separates information into individual sections or zones. Data can be stored in these sectors and read by the disk drive. A unit of storage of one or more sectors is called a cluster.

security the method of protecting files or programs so that unauthorized people cannot copy or access them. There are several methods of securing files, including the use of a PASSWORD, physically locking the computer, the use of data ENCRYPTION or by downloading files to removable disks for safe storage. Security is a major concern for computer users since a great deal of damage can be done to files or systems if someone has unauthorized access to a computer.

seek to locate a file on a disk. A FILE ALLOCATION TABLE indicates the part of the disk on which the file or program is stored. The READ/WRITE HEADS are directed to the correct location, and the information is read to the processor. The time that it takes for the read/write heads to reach the correct sector is called the **seek time**.

select to chose a portion of a document or database in which to perform a particular task or to review the selected records. The **selection** in the document may be made in order to change the text formatting or to move it from one part of the document to another. The selected records in a database of sales may be used to analyse results for a particular salesperson.

serial communication a method of transferring data over a single wire, one BIT at a time. Data can be transferred over a relatively long distance using serial communications compared with parallel communication, which is restricted to a distance of around three metres because of the problems of interference.

serial mouse an input pointing device that is connected to a serial port on the computer as opposed to the bus mouse, which is connected to the main processor board.

serial port a PORT on the back of a computer that is set up to allow SERIAL COMMUNICATIONS between the computer and another device.

serial printer a printer that connects to a serial port of the computer. The serial printer is slower than a parallel printer but can be sited at the other end of the office whereas the parallel printer must be within about three metres of the computer.

serif the detailed strokes at the end of the main strokes of a character. Times is a FONT with serifs. (*See also* SANS SERIF.)

server a computer used in a LOCAL AREA NETWORK that is the main source of programs or shared data. The server also controls the use of peripherals such as printers or modems by creating queues of requests that are answered in a sequential order.

service provider a company that provides a connection to the INTERNET in return for a monthly subscription and a charge per hour of use. The service provider may facilitate a simple connection or may make available added services such as news and sports services, on-line shopping, etc.

set up to install a piece of hardware or software into a computer system so that it works with the system. For example, when you buy a new program it has to be set up by creating the correct system files and by placing the various parts of the program in the correct directories on the storage disk. A scanner has to be set up by providing the correct connections to the computer and also by providing the correct software to operate the scanner.

shareware software that can be obtained on a trial basis but to continue to use the program a fee must be paid to the author. Shareware programs are copyrighted. Shareware can be obtained from a variety of sources but most commonly can be downloaded from an ON-LINE INFORMATION SERVICE such as Prodigy or America Online

sheet feeder a device that FEEDS individual pages of paper into a printer or a scanner. The paper is drawn through by a series of friction rollers. For printing, the sheet feeder is predominantly used on LASER PRINTERS and inkjet printers.

shell a UTILITY PROGRAM that operates as an INTERFACE between the user and an operating system that is regarded as difficult to use. For example, WINDOWS is a shell utility for DOS.

shift key a key on a keyboard that allows the user to select an alternative range of characters such as uppercase letters, brackets, pound signs, etc. The key is identified by a white, upward facing arrow or the word 'shift'.

shortcut key a key or more commonly a key combination that allows the user to bypass the normal menu selection process by pressing a key or keys simultaneously. The shortcut is used for commonly used commands such as cut and paste (Ctrl x and Ctrl v), open file (Ctrl o) or create new file (Ctrl n).

silicon the material from which computer chips are made. It is a naturally occurring semiconductor material found in sand and clay.

Silicon Valley an industrial area in the Santa Clara Valley in California that has a high concentration of information technology industries. It can also refer to an area with a concentration of information technology businesses. **Silicon Glen** is an area in central Scotland that has a similar cluster of information technology companies.

Sim City *see* EDUTAINMENT.

SIMM (Single Inline Memory Modules) a small plug-in circuit board that contains MEMORY chips required to add more RAM to a computer. (*See also* DIMM).

simulation an application based on assumptions about behaviour that can be used to produce a model of real life effects. For example, a business simulation can be produced on a SPREADSHEET to show a manager the effect that differing sales levels would have on profit or how advertising may affect sales. In the motor industry, a simulation of a wind tunnel can tell the designers the best shape for a new car design. The basic assumptions are important as they determine the accuracy of the simulation. The more assumptions, the more complex the model but the more accurate the results.

single density a disk storage technology that has been superseded because of the small amount of data that can be stored on the disk. The magnetic particles on the disk are relatively large compared with the much finer particles used in modern high density drives, which can typically hold about four times the amount of information.

single in-line package (SIP) a small circuit board similar to a SIMM. Because it is more difficult to install, it is usually installed by the computer manufacturer.

single sided disk an old type of storage disk that allows only one side to be used to read or write data. Most modern disks allow data to be written on both sides of the disk.

site licence an agreement between the authors of a computer program and a user of the program that allows the user to run the program on an agreed number of computers at one time.

slide show a preset list of graphic presentations that are displayed on a screen in a predefined order. The purpose of the slide show can vary from a sales presentation to a presentation for a directors' meeting.

slot *see* EXPANSION SLOT.

small cap or **small capital** a capital letter that is smaller than a normal capital. The cross-references in this book are in SMALL CAPS, while this is the NORMAL CAPITAL.

small computer system interface *see* SCSI.

smart terminal in a NETWORK of computers, a smart terminal is one that has its own processor and secondary storage. In a network, terminals do not need to be smart, they can be DUMB TERMINALS, in which case they have no processing power or storage other than that of the network server.

snail mail the term used by some to describe the postal service, which can take days to deliver a letter as opposed to the ELECTRONIC MAIL service which can deliver the mail instantly. Electronic mail is much faster as long as the recipient opens his or her computer mailbox.

soft a term used to describe a hyphen or PAGE BREAK inserted by a word processing, page layout or spreadsheet program, as opposed to a HARD command inserted by the user.

software any program that is loaded into a computer's internal memory and that tells the computer what function to perform. Software is also known as programs or applications.

software licence an agreement between the user of a program and its author that gives the user the right to use one copy of it. The user pays a fee for this facility. When payment has been made for the program, the user often considers that he or she has paid for it outright, but this is not the case. The user has paid for a licence to use the software and has not bought it.

software piracy the illegal, unauthorized copying of software. Since software can be copied very quickly, piracy is common and costs software publishers vast amounts of money. COPY PROTECTION can be incorporated in programs, but this often penalizes legitimate users, who require a program copy because of a disk failure, so it has become less common. Some analysts argue that as the cost of software reduces, piracy will decline as more people would rather pay a reasonable price for the official package with all the manuals and technical backup than have a pirated copy.

software publisher the company that writes, markets, sells and distributes a computer program. Major software publishers are Microsoft, Lotus, Word Perfect.

sort a command that organizes data into a particular order. The order can be alphabetical or numeric and can be ascending (from A to Z or 1 to 10) or descending (from Z to A or 10 to 1). A sort command is available in a wide range of applications.

sort key in a DATABASE MANAGEMENT PROGRAM the sort key is the FIELD name by which a SORT is to be conducted. For example, in a database of stock items the sort key could be by stock name or by stock code.

sort order the way in which a sort places data. The most common sort order is to use the ASCII character set. This is a set of 128 characters of the alphabet (upper and lower case) and numbers plus other characters such as ',. } {( )'.

sound board an add-on board for PERSONAL COMPUTERS that gives digital sound capabilities to a computer. MACINTOSH computers have stereo sound facilities built into the system so no added board is required.

source the file or disk from which information or data is taken by the processor. Once the processor has performed a task the data or information is sent to its destination disk or file.

source code the instructions that a programmer creates when writing a PROGRAM. It has to be translated or compiled into MACHINE CODE before the computer can run the program.

SPARC (Scaler Processor ARChitecture) a processor chip design by Sun Microsystems for computers that are used for CAD design work or other high power requirements.

special interest group a group of like-minded users who regularly get together to discuss their chosen topic on-line on an INTERNET connection.

speech recognition an information processing technology in which the spoken word is converted into signals that can be recognized by speech recognition software and converted into commands for the computer to follow.

speech synthesis the process by which the computer translates text into computer generated output that simulates human speech. This type of technology may assist visually impaired people to use computers.

spell checker a UTILITY PROGRAM or part of a larger application that individually checks each word in a document against a dictionary file. The spell checker can show the correct spelling of a word and a list of alternatives if it cannot recognize a word in the text. The chosen version is then inserted into the document.

spike a surge of electricity that at best causes a system CRASH or at worst can burn out components inside the computer. A device to protect against power surges can be bought and placed between the mains supply and the computer.

split screen a facility offered by some wordprocessing and spreadsheet programs that allows the screen to be divided in to two or four panels so that different parts of a document can be viewed at one time. This facilitates editing processes such as copying and pasting from one part of a document to another.

spooler a UTILITY PROGRAM that is used to facilitate printing. When the processor is sending information direct to the printer it must wait for the printer to deal with the output. Since the printer is significantly slower, the processor is not being used effectively. The processor can alternatively send the output to a spooler, which saves all the printing commands. The spooler saves the commands faster than the printer can process them so the processor is free to perform other tasks while the spooler communicates with the printer at the speed of the printer.

A spreadsheet window

spreadsheet a program that creates an on-screen worksheet, which is a series of ROWS and COLUMNS of CELLS into which values, text and formulae can be placed. The spreadsheet is recalculated whenever a change to a cell's value or formula is made. The original spreadsheet (Visicalc) was created in 1978 for use on an Apple II computer. Since then spreadsheets have become more and more sophisticated with database management, analytical graphics, statistical analysis and many more functions available. One of the main uses of spreadsheets is WHAT IF ANALYSIS. By creating a model of a business or economy, many variables can be input in turn to assess the effect of changes in values on the economy or business. Spreadsheets are a very effective tool for businesses of all sizes, for example, in the production of cash flow analysis.

SQL *see* STRUCTURED QUERY LANGUAGE.

SRAM (Static Random Access Memory) a fast but relatively expensive MEMORY that is used to create CACHES. Information put into SRAM is held there as long as the computer power is switched on. Information from SRAM can be accessed very quickly by the processor.

stand-alone a term applied to a computer system that is self-contained and has only the hardware and software required by the user.

standard a predefined set of guidelines that is set by the industry's manufacturers to determine the type of INTERFACE between a PERIPHERAL DEVICE and the computer and the way the device communicates with the processor.

standard mode an operating mode for MICROSOFT WINDOWS that speeds up the operation of Windows applications.

star dot star the colloquial name given to the WILDCARD search in DOS and WINDOWS. The use of *.* finds all files because the asterisk can represent any set of characters.

star network a representation of a NETWORK where the network SERVER is located in a central position and the user stations are connected around this central point. The terminals have no connection to one another, only to the server.

start bit the initial BIT sent in SERIAL COMMUNICATIONS that indicates to the receiving computer that the BYTE of data is about to be sent.

start-up disk a disk that contains the operating system code required to start the computer. The start-up disk is usually a hard disk but can be a floppy. Having a floppy disk as a start-up disk is very useful, especially if something happens to the hard disk that makes it unreadable.

start-up screen a Macintosh graphics file that, when placed in the START-UP DISK, will be displayed on start-up. Any picture can be used, from one of a car to one of the user.

stationery document *see* STYLESHEET.

stop bit the final BIT sent in SERIAL COMMUNICATIONS, which indicates to the receiving computer that the BYTE of data has been sent.

storage the retention of programs and data in a computer in such a way as to allow the computer processor to access the information when required. The primary storage is the RAM and ROM, and the SECONDARY STORAGE is a device such as an optical or magnetic drive.

street price the price at which a computer or other hardware can be bought as compared with the official retail price set by the manufacturer. The street price is usually below the recommended price since the resellers discount the goods in order to boost or maintain their sales volumes.

string a series of characters that can be used as a basis for a search. For example, the search string 'help' will bring up all occurrences of the word or part of a word 'help'.

structured programming language a computer programming language that encourages the programmer to think logically about the purpose of the program and to avoid the use of the GOTO statement (which can result in a messy unreadable program). The use of named procedures and branch control structures is encouraged. Examples of structured programming languages are C, PASCAL and ADA.

structured query language (SQL) a set of commands used

to assist users in obtaining information from a database.
SQL has 30 commands and is thus relatively easy to learn
and use. SQL can be used for querying databases in both
personal computers and mainframe computers.

stylesheet a file that has been saved with all the FORMATTING
required for a particular task. The stylesheet has all the required fonts, paragraph indents, font sizes and margins.
Stylesheets or stationery documents can be created for
many documents, such as standard letters, news sheets,
promotional fliers, monthly reports, etc.

stylus a device resembling a pen (with no ink) that is used as
an INPUT DEVICE on a GRAPHICS TABLET, screen or PERSONAL
DIGITAL ASSISTANT.

subdirectory a DIRECTORY within a directory. For example, a
main directory may be used to list correspondence that may
be grouped into two different areas—letters and memos.
The two subdirectories of the main directory would therefore be letters and memos. Letters may then have its own
subdirectories for different categories.

submenu a secondary MENU that appears as a set of OPTIONS
associated with an option chosen in the main menu. In a
GRAPHICAL USER INTERFACE environment using drop down
menus, the submenu appears to the side of the main menu
choices.

subscript text that is printed slightly smaller and below the
main body of text. The numbers in this chemical formula
are in subscript: $H_2 SO_4$

suite a collection of several programs that fit together to provide a comprehensive set of tools that a business person
may use. It should include a word processing program, a

spreadsheet, an organizer, a database, a communications program and a presentation program.

super computer a computer designed to execute very complex calculations at very high speeds. The type of problems that super computers are good at solving include weather forecasting, global warming analysis and economic analysis.

superscript text that is printed slightly smaller and above the main body of text. The numbers in the following are in superscript: $Y = X^2 + Z^3$

super VGA a GRAPHICS display STANDARD that can display from 800 pixels by 600 vertical lines to 1024 pixels by 768 lines with 256 colours.

surge protector a device placed between a computer and the mains power supply to protect the computer from momentary increases in the voltage of the power supply.

swap file a file used when a computer's RAM is not large enough to store the full program. A swap file is held on the hard disk, and the computer processor moves information between the RAM and the swap file as required.

synchronous a term used to describe a method of communication that is synchronized with electronic signals produced by a computer. A data BIT is sent with every tick of the computer. (*See also* PARALLEL PORT.)

syntax the set of rules that govern the way in which a command or statement is given to a computer so that it recognizes the command and proceeds accordingly.

syntax error an error resulting from the incorrect spelling of a command or in the way the commands are entered. For example, DOS commands must be entered in strict order of command first, then parameters and then switches.

SYSOP (SYStem OPerator) the person who is in charge of a BULLETIN BOARD or an area in an ON-LINE INFORMATION SERVICE. The SYSOP is responsible for helping users and ensuring that the rules of the bulletin board are maintained.

system or **computer system** all the necessary hardware and software required in an installation, all of which is interconnected and set up to work together (central processing unit, disk drives, monitor, printer, keyboard, and so on).

system 7 a version of the MAC OS, an operating system for the Macintosh range of computers.

system date the date that is held in a computer's internal memory. This memory is not subject to loss when the computer's power is switched off as it is protected by a battery backup.

system disk a disk containing the operating system and all related files. The system disk can be a floppy or a hard disk.

system error an error that occurs at the SYSTEM level of operation of a computer, as opposed to a user-generated error. System errors may be caused by bad programming.

system program *see* ROM.

system prompt an indicator to show that the OPERATING SYSTEM is ready to accept a command. The system prompt is seen in command line operating systems as opposed to GRAPHICAL USER INTERFACE systems. In DOS the system prompt is C> where **c** represents the current disk drive.

system software the group of codes that the computer requires to start up. It includes the OPERATING SYSTEM, which controls all the major functions of the computer.

T

tab key in a text editing program a key that is used to move text to the right by a fixed or preset number of spaces. The tab key can be used to indent the first line in a paragraph or to create a table of columns. The number of spaces that the text moves to the right is determined by the TAB STOPS. These can be set at any value. The tab key is also used to move the CURSOR between on-screen command OPTIONS.

table text that is arranged in rows and columns in order to display information. A table is also the basic structure for storage of data in DATABASE MANAGEMENT PROGRAMS. Rows correspond to records, and columns correspond to fields of data.

tab stop the point where the cursor stops when the tab key is pressed. Normally the tabs are preset at half an inch but can be altered to any value. There are normally four types of tab stops: left tab stop aligns the text to the left side of the tab stop; right tab stop aligns itself to the right of the tab stop; centre tab stop aligns the text centrally under the tab stop; decimal tab stop aligns the decimal point of a number under the tab stop.

tagged image file format *see* TIFF.

Tandy a major corporation that manufactures and sells a range of personal computers and electronic goods. Originally Tandy used its own OPERATING SYSTEM but since the mid-1980s has incorporated IBM compatibility into its computer systems (*see* COMPATIBLE).

tape a thin strip of plastic, coated with a magnetic recording material, that is normally held in a plastic case. It is used principally as a backup storage medium. It is not used for secondary storage because of the relatively long access time to retrieve data that is a long way into the tape. Data is held sequentially on the tape and since the tape is held on reels the last data to be saved to the tape is at the end of the reel. If the user wants to access the data at the end of the reel the tape drive must spin the reels from the start to the end of the tape. This could take several minutes thus precluding the tape drive as anything but backup storage.

target the destination for a copied file. A file is copied from a SOURCE to a target.

TB, tbyte *see* TERABYTE.

technical support the provision of information, usually by a telephone hotline, for registered users of hardware or software by the manufacturer if they have a problem. The support for the initial period after purchase is normally free of charge. After the initial period (often three months) the technical support is charged at a set rate per hour.

telecommunications the use of the telephone systems, either land lines or satellite, to transmit information (voice, video or computer data).

telecommute to work from a home base rather than commute to the office. Telecommuting has been made possible by the efficiency of the telephone systems. An employee can perform tasks at home and send results to the office computer by using a MODEM. In addition, messages can be transmitted to the employee at home through an ELECTRONIC MAIL system. It has been relatively slow to catch on since employees miss the social contact of work at the office and managers do not like the reduced supervision over workers who are not in the office. Where home working has grown is in subcontracted work as supervision is a lower requirement. People who work at home in this way are often called **teleworkers**. This is becoming more popular, and groups of teleworkers can work together on a large contract. Much work is undertaken for foreign companies, when advantage can be taken of time differences, e.g. to update records and have them ready for the next working day.

Telenet a commercial ON-LINE INFORMATION SERVICE that allows connection to other computers worldwide. Telenet is usually used as access to the INTERNET.

teleworker *see* TELECOMMUTE.

template a document that is prewritten and formatted and ready for final editing or adjustment before printing. For example, an invoice can be set up with all the headings, automatic date entry, formulae to calculate VAT, etc. The only data required before printing is the customer name, description of the goods or service provided and the amount.

tera (T) a prefix representing one trillion (10^{12}).

terabyte (TB, tbyte) a measurement of MEMORY capacity that is approximately equal to one trillion BYTES. The actual number is 1,099,511,627,776 bytes.

terminal an INPUT/OUTPUT device consisting of a monitor, keyboard and connection to a central server. A terminal can be a DUMB TERMINAL, which has no processor or secondary storage, or a SMART TERMINAL, which has these facilities and can thus operate on its own as well as operate as part of the NETWORK.

terminal emulation a procedure whereby a TERMINAL or PERSONAL COMPUTER acts like another in order that communications can take place between computers. Since there are many different types of personal computer, STANDARDS have been devised that allow the computers to communicate. These are incorporated into communication programs so that, for example, a home computer acts like the terminal of a large computer, which is the centre of an on-line service. Terminal emulations include TTY, VT42 and VT52.

text alignment the JUSTIFICATION of text in a word processing or page layout document. Text is aligned with reference to the right and left margins of the page. Text can be lined up with the right margin (unusual), the left margin (most common) the centre of the page (for headings) or can be fully justified (spread out so that the text reaches both the left and right margins).

text chart in business presentations a slide presentation that contains no graphics. The slide consists only of text, e.g. showing a menu list of items.

text editor a basic word processing program that is used mainly for writing computer programs and batch files. It has very limited facilities for formatting and printing.

text file a file that contains only ASCII characters. This file type is used mainly for transfer of information between different programs or computers. The file does not contain any formatting codes that could indicate bold or italic text or differing fonts or font sizes. The use of text files is diminishing as many programs have automated FILE TRANSFER procedures to allow one program to read a file created in another program.

text wrap *see* WRAP AROUND TYPE.

thermal printer a printer that uses heat to form an image on special paper. The thermal heads heat the paper, which has a wax-type coating causing a discoloration that results in print. Fax machines use this type of printing device. Despite its speed and quietness it is not popular, mainly because of the waxy feel of the paper.

thesaurus a book or file that lists alternative meanings for words, i.e. synonyms. Most word processing programs now include an electronic thesaurus that displays a list of synonyms for each word selected. Once the new word has been chosen, the program will replace the old word with the new.

third generation an era in computing around the mid 1960s when the transistor was replaced by INTEGRATED CIRCUITS and disk storage and ON-LINE terminals were introduced.

third party vendor a business that buys and sells computer equipment and accessories. The company buys from a computer manufacturer and sells to the end user (a business or the general public). The third party vendor makes life easier for the manufacturer, who does not need to worry about the selling or marketing function, and provides a point of contact for buyers, who can view and assess a range of equipment before purchase.

three-dimensional spreadsheet a SPREADSHEET program that consists of several layers of related pages or worksheets. For example, if a company has four shops, a worksheet can be created for each shop to show its income and expenditure. In order to produce a consolidation of the results of the

four shops a fifth worksheet is created that calculates the
sum of the figures for each shop. The formulae in this sheet
use three dimensional statements such as:

'= Shop1! \$C\$9 + Shop2! \$C\$9 + Shop3! \$C\$9 + Shop4! \$C\$9'

throughput a measure of a computer's overall speed of performance as opposed to the speed of a particular element of
the computer or system. The slowest component will effectively determine the performance of the computer. For example, a slow disk drive will counter the effect of a fast
processor chip. Similarly fast RAM and a RAM cache will be
useless if the chip is slow.

tick a single beat of the MICROCHIP that determines the
number of instructions that a chip can process. Normally a
chip can process one instruction per tick.

TIFF (Tagged Image File Format) a STANDARD relating to
graphic images. A TIFF file contains a series of dots (*see*
BITMAP) that makes up the image. The dots can be printed,
stored on a disk or displayed on a monitor.

tile to set windows in a side by side fashion on the desktop.
Tiling windows shrinks the size of the windows so that
more can be seen on the screen. Windows can be tiled or
shown as CASCADING WINDOWS.

time sharing a technique for sharing resources in a MULTI-
USER system. Users do not notice that they are sharing the
system resources. If the system does become overloaded
with users, they will notice a decline in the operating speed.

title bar a shaded bar containing the name of the file that is
found at the top of an on screen window in GRAPHICAL USER
INTERFACE systems. The title bar is shaded when the WINDOW
is active.

Title bar

toggle a key OPTION that allows switching back and forth between states of operation, i.e. the FUNCTION is switched on and off. The caps lock key is a toggle key that alternatively switches to uppercase mode and back to lowercase mode each time the key is pressed.

token passing a PROTOCOL in which tokens move around a NETWORK. When a NODE wants to send a message over the network it has to obtain a free token. The node that controls the token controls the network until the message has been passed and acknowledged.

token ring network a LOCAL AREA NETWORK that uses token passing technology as the basis for communications.

toner powdered ink that is electrically charged and is used in laser printers and photocopying machines. The toner is applied to a charged drum and fused to the paper with a heating element.

toolbar a strip of buttons that appears at the top of the screen that are used to select commands without using menus. The tool bars can be edited so that the user can choose the buttons that are most appropriate to the tasks that are being undertaken. Tool bars are commonly used in word processing and other software packages.

A sum button on the toolbar

toolbox a set of prewritten programs or routines used by programmers for incorporation into larger programs. This saves time and ensures that there is consistent implementation of the toolbox routines, such as printing.

top down programming a method of designing programs. It starts with a basic statement of the program's main objectives, which is then divided into sub-objectives, and so on. The sub-objectives or subcategories are of a type that can be programmed easily. C and PASCAL are STRUCTURED PROGRAMMING LANGUAGES that lend themselves to top down programming.

topology a LOCAL AREA NETWORK layout. Topologies can be centralized or decentralized. A centralized network is like a star and a decentralized network is like a ring.

touch sensitive display a type of screen with a pressure sensitive panel in front of the screen. The panel is effectively lined up with the display options, which are selected by pressing the panel at the correct place. This type of screen technology is used for public information access rather than in business.

tower system of style of computer system in which the electronics, disk drives, expansions cards, etc, are contained in a box resembling a tower that usually sits on the floor beside the user's desk. The VDU and keyboard sit on the desk. (*See also* MINI TOWER.)

tpi *see* TRACKS PER INCH.

track one of a number of concentric circles on a floppy or hard disk. The track is encoded on the disk during FORMATTING and is a particular area on the disk for data storage.

trackball an INPUT DEVICE that is similar to a mouse that is turned upside down. Instead of moving the mouse over the desk to move the ball, the ball is moved within a static unit. The trackball takes up less space on a desktop than a mouse, and in some NOTEBOOK COMPUTERS the trackball is embedded in the case of the computer.

trackpad an INPUT DEVICE that is a development of the trackball. It consists of a square pad embedded in the case of a LAPTOP COMPUTER, and movement of the finger over the pad moves the cursor on the screen.

tracks per inch (tpi) a measure of the density of data storage on floppy disks, higher figures representing a greater capacity for data.

tractor feed a mechanism, similar to PIN FEED, that is used in dot matrix printers to push the paper past the print head. The mechanism has sprockets that engage in prepunched perforations at the edges of the paper.

transfer to move information from disk to memory and vice versa.

translate to change a file that has been saved in one file format to another so that the file can be opened in a different program.

tree structure a way of organizing directories on a disk that shows the core or main directory at the top with the various subdirectories and sub-subdirectories shown like the branches of a tree extending downwards and outwards.

triple spin CD ROM a CD ROM drive that operates three times faster than a standard CD ROM drive. CD ROMs are relatively slow, and so manufacturers have attempted to speed up processing by spinning the drives faster.

Trojan horse a program that appears to perform a valid

function but, in fact, contains hidden codes that can cause damage to the system that runs the program. It does not replicate itself or infect other files as a VIRUS does.

troubleshoot to investigate the reason for a particular occurrence or malfunction in a computer system. Very often a failure is caused, not by a major problem, but a small error that can be rectified quite easily.

TrueType a font technology that rivals Postscript and displays on-screen fonts exactly as the printer prints them out. The fonts are SCALABLE and so, no matter which font size is chosen, the screen display and the printer will be the same. TrueType fonts do not require any special printer processors, unlike Postscript fonts, to enable them to be printed, and so the TrueType document is portable between systems.

truncate to cut off part of an entry (a number or character string) either to ensure that it fits a predefined space or to reduce the number of characters for easier processing.

tutorial a process of instructions that guides the user through a series of steps designed to show the features of a program such as a word processor, database or spreadsheet.

twain a STANDARD connected with scanning that allows a document to be scanned without leaving the application into which the image is to be inserted.

type ahead buffer a memory BUFFER that stores the characters being typed on the keyboard so that they can be processed by the RAM when the processor is free.

typeface a set of characters sharing a unique design, such as Courier or Times. Typefaces can be SERIF or SANS SERIF.

type style refers to the WEIGHT of type or the slope of the type as opposed to the size of the type or the typeface. The weight of type refers to how **bold** the type appears and the slope of type refers to whether *italic style* is chosen.

U

undelete program a UTILITY PROGRAM that is used to restore files that have been deleted from a disk, possibly by accident. The recovery (*see* RECOVER) of the file depends on there having been no other data written onto the disk since the file was deleted as this would affect the storage areas.

underline a command used to highlight text by placing a line under the selected word or portion of text. Double underline can also be used in some word processing packages.

undo a command available in programs that reverses the effect of the previous command given. It allows the user to cancel the effect of a command that has had an unforeseen or disastrous effect.

undocumented features of programs that have not been documented in the program manual.

unformatted a term indicating that an item MAGNETIC MEDIA requires FORMATTING prior to being put into operation.

uninterruptable power supply (UPS) a power supply that switches to an alternative power source, such as a battery, in the event of the main supply crashing. The alternative will probably have a short life but will be long enough to allow proper shutdown to take place, thus preserving data.

UNIX an OPERATING SYSTEM suitable for a wide range of computers from MAINFRAMES to PERSONAL COMPUTERS. It is suited to MULTIUSER situations and can handle MULTITASKING.

unprotected software software that can be copied from the original program disks on to other floppy disks or onto a hard disk. Retaining a copy of a program disk is sensible in case of damage to the original. Some software is protected so that copies cannot be taken, which can create problems if disk damage occurs (*see* COPY PROTECTION).

update to revise the contents of a file, usually a database file, so that the contents reflect the correct and current state.

upgrade to purchase the most recent version of software released by the author or to purchase a new hardware update, such as a new computer system.

upload to copy a file from your computer to another computer connected through the telecommunication system. (*See also* DOWNLOAD.)

uppercase type in capital letters as opposed to lower case.

THESE ARE UPPERCASE CHARACTERS
these are lowercase characters

upward compatibility the ability of an application program to run under a more advanced computer or operating system than it was originally designed for.

user the person who is operating the computer.

user-defined a selection of preferences chosen by the user of a computer.

user-friendly jargon for a system that is easy to learn and operate. A user-friendly program often involves the use of MENUS rather than commands that have to be remembered; help that is available on screen at the touch of a key; ERROR MESSAGES with some explanation of the fault and solution; PROMPTS when performing potentially damaging procedures, e.g. questions such as 'Do you really want to . . .' when deleting a file. Applications software also comes with numerous manuals including one presenting the basics of a program in a way that is easily understood.

Computers using GRAPHICAL USER INTERFACE are generally thought to be more user-friendly than those systems that rely on typed commands, e.g. DOS.

user group a gathering of people with similar objectives who communicate through computers.

user interface a means by which the user communicates with the computer. The different user INTERFACES include a GRAPHICS USER INTERFACE, in which the user communicates through MENUS and ICONS, and the command line interface in which the user has to type the appropriate command at a PROMPT.

utility program a program that helps the user to obtain the most benefit from a computer system by performing routine tasks, e.g. copying data from one file to another. (*See also* DESK ACCESSORY.)

V

V42 bis a data compression and error correction STANDARD used for communications between MODEMS.

vaccine a UTILITY PROGRAM designed to prevent a computer VIRUS from attacking a system. The vaccine has three things to do: prevent the virus attacking the system; detect the presence of a virus once it is in the system; remove the virus. Some vaccines do all three while others manage only one.

value a numeric CELL entry in a SPREADSHEET program. A value can be a constant that is entered directly into a cell or it can be the product of a formula.

vapourware software under development that is marketed in advance of its release. Often the release is delayed because of technical problems but the marketing goes on, creating the impression that the software does not exist.

VDT (Video Display Terminal) *see* VDU.

VDU (visual display unit) or **monitor** or **screen** or **video display terminal** a device that incorporates a cathode-ray tube and produces a picture of computer input or output. The display is created by firing a series of rays at a phosphorus-coated screen. The screen colours are created by mixing red, green and blue. There is some concern that the electromagnetic radiation given out by VDUs may be hazardous. They emit X-rays, ultraviolet radiation, electrostatic discharge and electromagnetic fields, but it is not proven that these emissions are dangerous to users. However, some studies have indicated that at a distance of 18 inches the radiation is less than that of the background, and this, and the use of low-radiation VDUs is being included in regulations for workers using computers.

vector graphics *see* OBJECT ORIENTED GRAPHICS.

verify a computer procedure that ensures that an operation was completed correctly.

version number the number assigned to a version or release of a program. Each time the author revises the program the version number is amended. Minor changes are indicated with a change in the decimal point while major changes are reflected in the main number.

VESA (Video Electronics Standards Association) a grouping of manufacturers who have devised STANDARDS to ensure that computers and VDUs are compatible.

video adapter the electronic card that generates the graphic output that is displayed on a VDU.

video card *see* **video adapter**.

video disk an optical storage device used for pictures, movies and sound. The disk has a high storage capacity holding up to two hours of TV pictures. Video disks can be used for interactive video when the disk is placed under the control of a computer.

video RAM *see* VRAM.

view an on-screen display of the contents of a file or part of a file. In DATABASE MANAGEMENT PROGRAMS a view can be generated to look at a selection of records. The selection depends on the criteria specified in a QUERY command.

virtual drive part of a computer's internal memory that is defined to act like a DISK DRIVE. Data can be stored temporarily in the virtual drive and accessed very quickly by the main processor.

virtual machine a computerized version of a computer that acts as if the computer was real and can actually run applications.

virtual memory (VM) the use of disk drive storage to extend the RAM of a computer. Because the processor treats virtual memory like RAM, the use of VM slows down the computer processing speed.

virtual reality a computer-generated environment that allows the user to experience various aspects of life without the travel or the danger that may be associated with the activities. A head-mounted display and sensor glove are used to create the effect.

virus a program that is designed to cause damage to systems that the virus infects. A virus program can copy itself from file to file and disk to disk and can therefore spread quickly through a computer system. It can also move between computers through the use of infected disks and also through telecommunication systems. A virus can be detected and removed by a VACCINE.

visual display unit *see* VDU.

voice/data switch a switch that identifies the type of call being received over a telephone line and that routes the call to the appropriate device. Voice calls go to a telephone and fax calls to a fax machine.

voice mail a system that stores voice communication on disk and can replay the message on command. Voice mail systems can be combined with telephone systems to provide computerized answer machines.

voice recognition the ability of a computer to recognize a voice, translate it into a digital pattern and reproduce the pattern as text or as computer generated speech. Voice recognition has improved in recent years, but voice recognition programs are still limited to several hundred words and require considerable training to recognize properly a user's speech.

voice synthesis *see* SPEECH SYNTHESIS.

volatile storage storage of which the contents are lost when power is removed, e.g. the RAM.

volume label a name that identifies the disk. The name is given when the disk is formatted (*see* FORMAT).

VRAM (Video RAM) RAM used in conjunction with a video card together to enhance the performance of video displays.

W

WAIS (Wide Area Information Server) an application that is used to search the thousands of databases connected to the INTERNET for a selection of keywords. It would be totally impractical to search the Internet manually for a particular reference so an automated program is used to perform the search.

wait state the interval programmed into a computer during which the MICROPROCESSOR waits for the RAM to catch up. As processors are built to run at faster speeds, the memory must be designed to keep up. If this does not happen then the faster processors will be worthless.

wallpaper an on-screen design that acts as a backdrop to the ICONS, WINDOWS, etc. GRAPHICAL USER INTERFACE computer operating systems have facilities to change the patterns through CONTROL PANELS.

WAN *see* WIDE AREA NETWORK.

warm boot a system restart that is initiated usually because a system error has occurred during operations. A warm boot will reset the memory and reload the OPERATING SYSTEM but may not reset PERIPHERAL DEVICES such as modems. A complete power shutdown and restart may be required for such operations. (*See also* BOOTSTRAPPING).

weight the relative thickness and thinness of type. Different TYPE STYLES can have different weights and within a particu-

lar style the weight can be graduated between extra light
and extra bold.

what if analysis a procedure using a SPREADSHEET to explore
the effect of changes in one input into a calculation. For example, what will happen to profits if volumes of sales are
increased by reducing the selling price?

			£		
Sales			80,000		
Cost of sales			30,000		
Gross Profit		62%	50,000		
Fixed Overheads			30,000		
Profit			20,000		
Using "What if" analysis we can find the effect of a change					
in sales on the profit					
Sales			60,000	100,000	
Profit			7,500	32,500	

Simple what if analysis

wide area network (WAN) a computer NETWORK that connects computers over long distances using telephone lines
or satellite communications. A wide area network can span
the world whereas a LOCAL AREA NETWORK can cover only a
few kilometres.

wild card a special character that is substituted for another
character or range of characters in a search of FILENAMES. In
DOS, an asterisk is a substitute for a number of characters
while a question mark is a substitute for one character. For
example, a search for *ook will find book, look, shook, and

so on, whereas a search for ?ook will find book and look, but not shook.

Winchester a type of HARD DISK used for data storage.

window an on-screen frame, usually rectangular in shape, that contains the display of a file. Several windows can be open on a desktop at a time. For example, two different files in a word processor may be open along with a window in a database management program.

Windows (Microsoft Windows) a comprehensive software facility that utilizes the GRAPHICAL USER INTERFACE features that were once the domain of the MACINTOSH. These include PULL-DOWN MENUS, a variety of accessories and the powerful facility of moving text and graphics from one program to another via the CLIPBOARD (an area for temporarily storing items that have been copied from one area, and that are to be pasted elsewhere). It is possible to run several programs at once, each within a separate window, and to move from one to the other very quickly. All applications that run within the Windows system have a common way of working with windows, dialog boxes, etc.

wizard a computerized EXPERT SYSTEM that leads the user through the sometimes complex process of creating a document such as an advertising flyer or a newsletter.

word count a feature of many programs that provides the user with a total number of words contained in a document. It is an invaluable feature of word processing programs.

Word Perfect a popular word processing program written by the Word Perfect Corporation.

word processing a method of document preparation, storage and editing, using a microcomputer/personal computer.

Word processing is the most widespread computing application, primarily because of the ease with which documents can be amended before printing. It is used to create, edit, format and print documents. This type of application is one of the most popular to be used on a desktop computer. The main software programs include Word Perfect, Word, AMIPro and MacWrite.

word wrap a feature of word processing programs that automatically moves words down to the next line if they go beyond the right-hand margin.

Word wrap takes the text automatically to the next line when the text goes beyond the right-hand margin.

Word wrap takes the text automatically to the next line when the text goes beyond the right-hand margin.

The right-hand margins are different, thus the text wraps at a different place

workbook a three-dimensional SPREADSHEET.

work group a small group of employees assigned to work together on a specific project. The work group can become more productive if personal computer technology is used to its best effect, i.e. if LOCAL AREA NETWORKS, ELECTRONIC MAIL, shared databases, and so on, are utilized.

worksheet a matrix of rows and columns in a SPREADSHEET program into which are entered headings, numbers and formulae.

workstation a desktop computer in a LOCAL AREA NETWORK

that serves as an access point to the network. Programs can be run from the workstation, and all network resources can be accessed.

worldwide web a HYPERTEXT-based document retrieval system linked to the INTERNET. Each page is indexed and can be linked to a related document. The worldwide web is allowing easier access to information available on the Internet.

WORM (Write Once Read Many) an OPTICAL DISK drive that can store up to one TERABYTE of data. Once the data is written to the disk it cannot be altered or erased.

wrap around type type that is contoured so that it surrounds a graphic item in a document. This is a feature of desktop publishing programs such as PageMaker, where it is called text wrap.

write an operation of the CENTRAL PROCESSING UNIT that records information on to a computer's RAM. It more commonly refers to the recording of information on to SECONDARY STORAGE media such as disk drives.

write/protect to protect a file or disk so that a user cannot modify or erase its data. A write/protect tab can be seen in the bottom right-hand corner of the back of a floppy disk, which, when slid down, protects the disk in this fashion.

WYSIWYG (What You See Is What You Get) the feature that what is seen on the screen is exactly what is replicated when the information is printed.

XYZ

x-axis the horizontal axis of a GRAPH. The horizontal axis usually contains the categories of values being plotted. For example, creating a graph of monthly sales will require that time be plotted on the horizontal or *x*-axis and sales be plotted on the vertical or *y*-axis.

x-y plotter a printer that creates a drawing by plotting *x* and *y* coordinates provided by the application program. This type of drawing is high precision and is commonly used for CAD drawings, architectural drawings and blueprints.

xmodem an asynchronous file transfer protocol that facilitates error-free transmission of computer files through the telephone system.

XMS (e*X*tended *M*emory *S*pecification) a set of guidelines that standardize the method a programmer can use to access memory above 1024 KILOBYTES, which is the memory limit associated with Intel 8088 and 8086 microchips.

XON/XOFF a method of communicating between MODEMS, whereby software controls the flow of data. In order that the two modems do not send data at the same time, one indicates that it wishes to send data by sending an XON code, and when it is finished it sends an XOFF code. *See also* COMMUNICATIONS SETTINGS.

YMCK an abbreviation for yellow, magenta (red), cyan (blue) and black, which are the basic colours used in printing.

ymodem an asynchronous file transfer protocol that is similar to xmodem but sends files in batches of 1024k as opposed to 128k.

z-axis represents the third dimension in a three-dimensional graphic image. The third dimension represents depth.

zap to delete or get rid of a program or file from a computer memory.

Zapf Dingbats a set of decorative symbols developed by Herman Zapf, a German TYPEFACE designer.

zip to COMPRESS files so that they utilize less space on a disk.

zone a subgroup of networked computers in a LOCAL AREA NETWORK. Messages or ELECTRONIC MAIL can be addressed to everyone in the subgroup.

zoom either to enlarge a window in order that it fills the screen or to enlarge or reduce the size of a page so that the full page can be seen on screen (**zoom out**) or the enlarged detail of the information in a smaller area can be seen (**zoom in**).

zoom box a small box positioned at the edge of a screen window that is used to ZOOM a window.

This is a zoom box on the window title bar